Your Own Terms

YOUR OWN
TERMS

A WOMAN'S GUIDE TO
TAKING CHARGE OF ANY NEGOTIATION

YASMIN DAVIDDS, PsyD

with ANN BIDOU

AMACOM

AMERICAN MANAGEMENT ASSOCIATION

New York • Atlanta • Brussels • Chicago • Mexico City • San Francisco
Shanghai • Tokyo • Toronto • Washington, D.C.

Bulk discounts available. For details visit: www.amacombooks.org/go/specialsales
Or contact special sales: Phone: 800-250-5308 Email: specialsls@amanet.org
View all the AMACOM titles at: www.amacombooks.org
American Management Association: www.amanet.org

This publication is designed to provide accurate and authoritative information in regard to the subject matter covered. It is sold with the understanding that the publisher is not engaged in rendering legal, accounting, or other professional service. If legal advice or other expert assistance is required, the services of a competent professional person should be sought.

LIBRARY OF CONGRESS CATALOGING-IN-PUBLICATION DATA
Davidds, Yasmin.
Your own terms : a woman's guide to taking charge of any negotiation /
Yasmin Davidds, PsyD with Ann Bidou.
pages cm
Includes bibliographical references and index.
ISBN 978-0-8144-3602-8 (pbk. : alk. paper) -- ISBN 978-0-8144-3603-5 (ebook)
1. Negotiation in business. 2. Negotiation. 3. Businesswomen. I. Bidou, Ann. II. Title.
HD58.6.D38 2015
658.4'052082--dc23   2015009457

About AMA

American Management Association (www.amanet.org) is a world leader in talent development, advancing the skills of individuals to drive business success. Our mission is to support the goals of individuals and organizations through a complete range of products and services, including classroom and virtual seminars, webcasts, webinars, podcasts, conferences, corporate and government solutions, business books, and research. AMA's approach to improving performance combines experiential learning—learning through doing—with opportunities for ongoing professional growth at every step of one's career journey.

Printing number

10 9 8 7 6 5 4 3 2 1

To the Davidds women in my family,
who live life on their own terms

My loving Mami, for your unconditional love; my beautiful sister Judy, for your constant strength and support; my soul sister Karina, for your protection up above the clouds; my beloved daughter, Divina, for your love that is so pure and precious; and my adorable nieces Isabella and Gabriella, whose presence brightens my life.

and

To the amazing alumni of the
Latina Global Executive Leadership Program

Your commitment to the program and to each other made my dream come true. Your constant love and support for one another provided each of you with unlimited strength and undeniable courage. May paying it forward sustain the power of the sisterhood.

Contents

Part 2: Build Leverage with Your Negotiation Toolbox

Acknowledgments

My journey in life has brought me across wonderful people and beautiful souls. I would like to acknowledge those who have supported me, inspired me, and nurtured me while I wrote this book. I honor you with my deepest gratitude:

Ann Bidou, my co-author, for giving such a powerful voice to my thoughts. You are the most amazing co-writer I have ever worked with. I feel blessed to have found you.

My literary agent, Linda Konner, for all your support and dedication to making this book possible.

The AMACOM team: Ellen Kadin, Ellen Coleman, Robin Perlow, Irene Majuk, Erika Spelman, and the entire editorial, production, sales, publicity, and marketing teams. Thank you all for believing in me and giving me the opportunity to share my message through this book.

The women and men who allowed me to share their voices with the world through our interviews: Dr. Betty Uribe, Graciela Meibar, Julius E. Robinson, and Pablo Schneider.

The only man in our family—my brother-in-law, Michael Wright—thank you for loving, honoring, and supporting the Davidds women even when we drive you crazy.

Ann Bidou wishes to thank Shoya Zichy, the co-author of her earlier books, *Career Match* and *Personality Power*, for recommending her for this job. Shoya, I have learned so much from you, and you will see your wisdom sprinkled throughout. Deepest thanks to Linda Konner, our agent, for bringing me to-gether with one of the most remarkable, brilliant, and gracious ladies I have ever met—my co-author, Yasmin Davidds. Linda—a very astute negotiator—is one of the few women I know who does not need to read this book at all! Warmest thanks to Brenda Nielson for her feedback on each chapter draft. I owe a huge debt of gratitude to Emily Hennessey and Sabrina O'Brien for helping to keep my other business going while writing distracted me. Finally, I wish to recognize the uncountable times my husband, Greg Bidou, sup-ported me through this writing period with unfailing encouragement, humor, and strength. Yes, ladies, there really are perfect husbands out there to be had, and I say my prayers of gratitude every day for having found one!

PART ONE

OWN YOUR GAME

Empowerment

1. The act of investing yourself with power
2. The process of enabling or permitting yourself the right to succeed
3. The ability to control your own destiny
4. The strength to maximize your own potential
5. The determination to define life on your own terms

1

Empower Yourself

This is not a book about how to become a barracuda at the bargaining table. It's definitely not a book about how to negotiate more like a man, or how to win by making others lose face or power. It is a book about leveraging those feminine strengths, such as nurturing and collaboration, that all people, men and women, respond to positively.

We women frequently feel like we're placed in a no-win situation before a negotiation even begins. If we make concessions to further the deal, we're viewed as weak; but if we go in strong for what we want, we're called unflattering names that often begin with "b." Either way, professional working relationships sustain damage. Where's the middle ground?

I live and work in the middle ground. I am an internationally known, bestselling author, a women's empowerment and negotiation specialist, and an expert in the world-renowned Karrass negotiation program. As one of the leading female negotiation experts in the United States and Latin America, I have trained thousands of corporate leaders in more than two hundred blue chip companies in twenty-two countries in the art and skill of negotiation. My clients range from senior judges to tribal leaders, from unionized prison guards to accountants, and from railroad officials to diplomatic trainees.

Based on these personal experiences and successes, I will teach you what I've taught others—how to be both a winning and a graceful negotiator. I will show you how you have more power at the negotiating table than most men, *without* resorting to sexual nuance. And I will help you realize that being a successful negotiator means that people end up liking you more, not less.

Let's begin by busting some myths.

Myth #1: Nice girls finish last. How do we get people to think we're "nice"? Parents teach their daughters it's by giving to others (while telling their sons it's more important to be strong and tough). Some parents model this by sacrificing what they want so others (particularly their children) can have what they want. At the bargaining table, being "nice" in this way often leads you to make too many concessions in return for too little. The goal is to get what you want, and leave others feeling like they won, too.

Myth #2: Emotions have no place in serious negotiations. Quite the contrary. Your emotions are a critical barometer for creating a win-win. There can't be a win-win unless *you* win, too. Women fear losing control emotionally and looking weak in the heat of negotiating. But to repress emotion requires tremendous amounts of energy, leaving little for strategic maneuvering. Emotions are energy that needs to be directed. You can't really control what emotions pop up, but you can control how you express them. Fear, for example, can be directed into the courage to walk into (or out of) the conference room, anger into setting reasonable boundaries, self-doubt into taking a calculated risk.

Myth #3: You have to be mean or angry to earn respect. One archetype of Western patriarchal cultures is the man who uses anger and bullying to force other, weaker people to do his bidding. Kings and conquerors, slave owners, and shop foremen are all examples. But a modern woman who uses such men as her role models rarely gains respect from her colleagues (or herself). What's the new paradigm? Earn respect from others by building your self-respect. This means taking a gracious and firm stand for what you desire.

Myth #4: You don't deserve to have it all; and if you push for it, people think you are selfish or unrealistic. Don't believe it for even one second! Who told you that you don't deserve to have what you want? When was the very first time you remember hearing this? How often did you hear it growing up? Did the person saying it have an agenda that would benefit him or her if you didn't get what you wanted? It may make no sense to honor at age thirty-six what your mother said you couldn't have at age six. As an adult, you are entitled to more! Pushing yourself to get more at first may feel fake and unnatural. But small, daily successes will start to translate into success in bigger arenas—asking for pay raises, buying a house, getting investors for your business, buying a used car, and even dealing with your ex-husband's divorce lawyer.

Myth #5: People don't like women who say "no." Users, manipulators, and exploiters certainly don't. Others will try to work within the reasonable boundaries that you set—and respect you for having them. I will teach you some critical skills for dealing with the users in a strong and confident manner so you walk away from the negotiation liking yourself and feeling little concern if the manipulators and exploiters don't.

Myth #6: Being a powerful woman who wins is OK for movie and TV characters, but in the real world it turns people off. The assumption here is that if a woman wins, colleagues—and sometimes even friends—are intimidated and turned off. Of course, if you always lose to someone, you may become afraid to deal with that person, which also is a turn-off. Instead, I will show you the art of being a powerful woman—someone who knows how to create win-win situations—without ever compromising your authentic femininity, by which I mean your ability to nurture, cooperate, and collaborate with respect for others and for yourself. You will draw others to you, gain respect and lifelong friendships along the way, and get what you want as well.

Isn't that who you want to be?

To start, let's agree on some definitions:

- *Negotiation*, so goes the old definition, is a game with rules of engagement. If you know the rules and employ them adroitly, you can win. Many of these rules—mostly developed by men—go counter to the collaborative approach most women prefer.

To change this game, we need to redefine it.

- *Negotiation*, newly defined, is a process whereby agreement is reached through discussion and compromise. Every interaction, no matter the context, no matter the scale, is a negotiation. It requires a mindset, tools, and a definable goal, all of which a woman can acquire with minimal skill and some practice.
- *Femininity*: The traits most often found and valued in females, such as gentleness, delicacy, and a nurturing attitude. These traits can produce tremendous gains when strategically applied to a negotiation.
- *Winning*: Winning means getting what you want. For some women, a one-sided win in their favor may create a momentary rush, but, for most, it ultimately doesn't sit as well as a win-win.

Transform How You Think and Feel

Let's begin. Here's how to own your game, live life at work and at home on your own terms, and never "get played" again.

1. **It starts in your head.** To achieve real, lasting, powerful results—to completely transform your quality of life—you must ask new questions, take new actions, get new results, and thereby gain new perspectives. At first, this will feel like putting on stiff new shoes. You will likely take them off and put them back on a few times before they start to feel right. Stay with it. You'll soon feel more comfortable.

2. **It starts with your heart.** You have the desire to become a master negotiator, without being heavy-fisted or cutthroat. Central to achieving this is facing the fear of losing friendships, respect, or

cooperation; the fear of disliking yourself; the fear of disobeying, being disloyal to, or being better than your parents. These are monumental, and there's no getting around the courage you will be required to muster. To conquer your fears requires consistent, powerful, strategic action—to trust that stepping up to the plate will dispel, and not reinforce, your fears. As your successes pile up, new, powerful, and positive beliefs and attitudes will lead to even greater results and momentum.

Together, we'll compress decades of effort into months (or even days) and make goals you considered merely dreams your daily reality. Don't allow your fears to hold you back!

Thirty-One Ways to Negotiate a Win-Win Solution

I can give you lists of tips and tricks (which I will), but the easiest way to absorb them is to see them in action. What follows is the story of Cathy's job and salary negotiation with Tom, showing how she successfully brought it to a win-win conclusion.

Once you've read the story, I suggest that each day you choose several of Cathy's strategies (in bold) and practice them until they become habitual.

1. **Power image management—show power externally.**[1] Cathy walked into GDW Company with her head high, her shoulders back, and a smile that would illuminate any room. Her navy blue suit was sharp and her hair was perfectly wrapped in a bun. She had interviewed for the national sales director position with the company and had been called back for what she hoped was the last interview. Today she was to meet with the executive vice president of sales, Tom Hernandez, the man to whom she would report if she got the position.

2. **Manage your expectations.**[2] She was excited about the possibilities but didn't want to get her hopes up too high. Before she entered

GDW's offices, she stood outside the door, closed her eyes, and took a deep breath.

3. **Go in with collaborative intentions.** "I intend to collaborate fully and create value for them and for me," she whispered to herself.

4. **Manage your emotions—turn raw emotion into positive action.**[3] She took one more deep breath and opened the door. She was greeted by Ann, an executive assistant seated behind a desk: "Mr. Hernandez is waiting for you; you can go right in." Cathy smiled as she opened the door. Tom Hernandez was sitting across the room at his desk and looked up when she entered. "You must be Cathy. You can take a seat right over there," he said, pointing to a small black leather chair stationed in front of his desk.

   "Thank you, Mr. Hernandez."

   "Please, call me Tom."

5. **Scan the room.** Cathy walked over to his desk, and as she extended her hand to formally introduce herself she glimpsed an 8 × 10 photo in an expensive frame showing two children and a beautiful, elegant woman.

6. **Find common ground.**[4] "It's a pleasure to meet you, Tom," Cathy said. She shook his hand firmly yet graciously and then indicated the frame on his desk.

7. **Test your assumptions.**[5] "Is that your family?" she asked.

8. **Scan for emotional response.** "Yes, it is," Tom said with a big grin on his face.

9. **Invoke positive feelings authentically.** "You have a beautiful family." "Thank you." Tom said in a proud voice as he took a seat in his black leather executive chair. (**Again, scan for emotional response.**)

10. **Identify power tactics.**[6] Once seated, Cathy noticed that her chair was much lower than Tom's, which was higher than most chairs and had big cushions and large armrests. "Is this a power tactic?" she thought to herself. In competitive (rather than collaborative) negotiations, it is common practice to seat the opponent in uncomfortable, lower chairs to convey symbolic power "over" the opponent.

11. **Counter or dismiss the tactic.** Cathy didn't allow the tactic to distract her. She was there with collaborative intent, determined to create value for all parties involved.

    (Note: You'll find an in-depth discussion of power tactics and how to counter them in Chapter 9.)

12. **Set and manage the environment with your attitude.**[7] Cathy's energy was solid, and the room felt light and pleasant. Had she been ruffled by the tactic, she would have taken a deep breath, sat up straight, put her feet on the ground, and looked the part of a strong candidate until she actually felt like one.

13. **Identify the low anchor offer.**[8] "Cathy," Tom began, "everyone here at GDW is impressed by you. They're very excited about your expertise and how it can contribute to the company. Let me not beat around the bush. We'd like you to join our team as national director of sales. The salary range is $105K to $115K. Because of your past experience, we don't want to start you at $105, yet we do need to leave some room for growth so we're going to start you at $110K."

14. **Identify and manage your emotions.**[9] Cathy was surprised by the low number but didn't allow her disappointment to show.

15. **Show your surprise.**[10] Instead, she flinched and said, "Are you sure that's accurate, Tom?" (Note: Cathy was in control of her emotions and allowed herself to flinch in order to make a statement.) "Of course it's accurate. Why wouldn't it be?"

16. **Allow the other party to save face.**[11] "I'm sure it's just an error. Human resources departments have so much going on, sometimes things like this happen." Tom actually had no idea what the median pay for the position was. "I'll have Ann check with human resources about this."

17. **Bring conversation back to the topic.**[12] "However, if the starting offer is $118K, I would be very interested in the position." Cathy has graciously set a new starting anchor.

18. **Set targets.**[13] Cathy had set her target salary for $130K plus sales development for her team.

19. **Prepare your concessions.**[14] Given Tom's low starting offer ($110K), asking for $130K would be too great a stretch.

20. **Analyze and defer risk.**[15] Going for $130K could strain what looked to be a positive relationship with her future boss.

21. **Know when to play it safe.**[16] She thought it best to play it safe and find another way.

22. **Shift the focus.**[17] "I have a few questions, Tom," Cathy said.

23. **Ask a leading question.**[18] "If I were to take the position, I would have a team, correct?" "Yes, you would have a team of six reports," said Tom. "You'd be inheriting one hell of a team. They are a focused and ambitious group, never settling for second best."

24. **Show appreciation.**[19] "That's great, Tom! I will need Grade A players to reach the kind of goals I'm thinking of."

25. **Read the other person's emotional response to determine next steps.** Tom looked surprised yet curious. "Really?" he said with an expectant smile.

    "Well, there are options and different numbers we can meet, yet that would depend on several things."

    "What do you have in mind?" Tom asked, intrigued.

    "To up the team's game and increase revenue by 4 percent and also decrease costs by 5 percent in the next six months would require the team members to work twelve-hour days for at least five months, after which they'd get a vacation and, based on our results, we can devise a new long-term strategy."

26. **Offer a strategic concession.**[20] Although that would be difficult for me, too, because I spend evenings with my children, for a period of five months, I would definitely be willing to hire a nanny to bring the kids to the office several evenings a week; the other evenings the team could just meet at my place.

27. **Tie a string to your concession.**[21] We're talking about nanny fees of $5K for five months. If the company is willing to pick up these costs, I'm sure I can motivate the team to put in the extra time to reach our numbers."

28. **Respond to body language.**[22] Seeing that Tom is receptive to the idea, Cathy went on, "If we really wanted to take our game up two levels and maximize the team's talents, I believe we can increase

Thirty-One Surefire Strategies to Get to Win-Win

1. Power image management—show power externally.
2. Manage your expectations.
3. Go in with collaborative intentions.
4. Manage your emotions—turn raw emotion into positive action.
5. Scan the room.
6. Find common ground.
7. Test your assumptions.
8. Scan for emotional response.
9. Invoke positive feelings authentically.
10. Identify power tactics.
11. Counter or dismiss the tactic.
12. Set and manage the environment with your attitude.
13. Identify the low anchor offer.
14. Identify and manage your emotions.
15. Show your surprise.
16. Allow the other party to save face.
17. Bring conversation back to the topic.
18. Set targets.
19. Prepare your concessions.
20. Analyze and defer risk.
21. Know when to play it safe.
22. Shift the focus.
23. Ask a leading question.
24. Show appreciation.
25. Read the other person's emotional response to determine next steps.
26. Offer a strategic concession.
27. Tie a string to your concession.
28. Respond to body language.
29. Win concessions for team to build loyalty.
30. Show confidence; build credibility.
31. Reset target.

revenue by 8 percent and reduce costs by 10 percent, for a total revenue increase of 18 percent."

"And what would that require?" Tom asked.

29. **Win concessions for team to build loyalty.** "Well, that would require the team working weekends for five months, so we would have to find a way to compensate them, and we would have to double the nanny's hours and pay."

"What makes you so sure you can reach these kinds of numbers?" Tom asked.

30. **Show confidence; build credibility.**[23] "Because I've done it before when I worked for Ace Corporation."

31. **Reset target.** "What would you be willing to pay someone to deliver those numbers?"

He smiled and said, "I can tell you that person would not be disappointed."

"Are we talking about $135K?" Cathy asked.

"With numbers like those, absolutely," Tom replied.

The Keys to Collaborative Negotiation

Cathy did well. Her approach was designed to create a win-win, and she succeeded in doing that for herself and for Tom. Their working relationship is off to a strong and positive start.

COMPONENTS OF A SUCCESSFUL COLLABORATIVE NEGOTIATION

"Collaborative" is one of several styles of negotiation (more on this in Chapter 5). It involves two parts:

1. *Value creation,* which changes the structure of the deal in a way that generates new value to make the deal both different and better (Cathy and Tom's new value was an increase in revenue).
2. *Value sharing,* which divvies up a share of resources such as dollars, goods, and services (Cathy's twelve-hour days, Tom's salary offer, additional staff compensation).

What do most people negotiate for? Dollars, goods, and services are merely assets that serve needs. People want their needs satisfied; although the assets are the tool, the ultimate goal is satisfaction. Satisfaction is hard to quantify because it can also be created by intangibles; it's not just the deal you make, it's how you make the deal. If you make a bigger pie, that creates tangible value. If you create psychological value, there is a greater appreciation of the deal. Both create satisfaction.

Women often operate on the assumption that when we agree quickly, we're providing satisfaction. Actually, we're doing the opposite. Saying "yes" too quickly *reduces* the sense of "winning" and, therefore, satisfaction. You value something more when you have to work for it! So make no mistake: *Collaboration does not mean quick capitulation.*

The collaborative style of negotiation is not "split the difference when there's a gap" negotiating. It's creating new value (a bigger pie, more satisfaction) through broader, out-of-the-box thinking.

FIVE TECHNIQUES TO CREATE COLLABORATIVE WIN-WINS

Here are some tactics you can use to create collaborative win-wins. They should be deployed when you need to establish trust and create a long-term relationship in addition to accomplish a specific goal:

1. **Ask in-depth questions to determine underlying interests.** Don't just react emotionally to the first demand; probe to find its motivation. Addressing underlying issues directly can open the door to flexible adjustment.
2. **At the beginning, try to identify common ground.** Leave the areas where you feel further apart for later. They'll be easier to resolve once you've established a pattern of agreeing.
3. **Always make sure comparisons are apples-to-apples.** Don't take your negotiating partner's word for this. Examine actual details of others' offers. Then keep the negotiation friendly and nonjudgmental: "Perhaps they didn't tell you . . . ." "You may not be aware of these hidden details . . . ."

4. **Don't let precedents or previous responses dictate current actions.** Making new history together is a wonderful way to cement a working partnership. "It may always have been done that way, but this way will boost profit without adding expense."

5. **If they get one, you get one.** Concessions—you will make them, guaranteed. But women often walk away feeling one-down—they concede, but the other party doesn't. Get in the habit of asking for something specific as payment for your concession. Don't concede for free, and don't expect the other party to volunteer anything. "I'll save you the cost of an extra ticket on your London trip, dear, if you arrange a Florida getaway in the fall." Both parties should gain.

The most natural negotiation strategy for women is the collaborative win-win. (In Chapters 7 and 8, I'll help you deal with competitive partners who don't want to play nice.)

Discover Your Personal Values: Core Negotiation Principles

There is one last, but very important, thing you need to do before moving on. Throughout this book, I'm going to help you become deeply aware of your personal values. Why? These shape the fundamental nature of what you want and what you are willing to do to get it. Values shape boundaries. They also fuel your passion to accomplish great things.

Take a moment now to do this values-defining exercise:

Work through the following list, quickly putting check marks next to any values that are part of your core negotiation values. As you do this, try not to check values that you believe are desirable and noble if they are not values you express in negotiations.

❐ Self-sufficiency	❐ Faithfulness	❐ Inclusiveness
❐ Fun	❐ Duty	❐ Individuality
❐ Fulfillment	❐ Practicality	❐ Fair play
❐ Honor	❐ Compassion	❐ Freedom

- ❏ Ambition
- ❏ Influence
- ❏ Learning
- ❏ Humility
- ❏ Wealth

- ❏ Happiness
- ❏ Change
- ❏ Responsibility
- ❏ Teamwork
- ❏ Authority

- ❏ Creativity
- ❏ Achievement
- ❏ Security
- ❏ Openness
- ❏ Objectivity

2

Your Style: Changes You Need to Make When Negotiating with Men or Women

By the time I had spent seven years working as a negotiation instructor and consultant for the Karrass Company, the leading global negotiation training company in the world, I'd spoken to thousands of executives. Teaching negotiation skills to Fortune 500 executives in the United States, Latin America, and Mexico had become second nature to me. I was good at it. No one ever challenged my competency. But that changed the day I walked into the boardroom of a large country club in Mexico to teach a negotiation course. Eighteen executive-level men (who were twice, if not triple, my age) dressed in expensive suits smiled at me but watched the door, expecting someone else to arrive after me.

"Buenos días, señorita," said one of the men pleasantly. "Where is the negotiation instructor?" Another man asked, "Are you his secretary?" I smiled, said hello, and in a pleasant yet assertive voice responded, "No, gentlemen, I'm not the secretary, I am the negotiation instructor." They chuckled and then, sounding more concerned, asked, "Where is the negotiation instructor?" Once again, with a smile but also using a stern voice I responded, "Seriously, gentlemen, I am the instructor."

As they looked at one another, their faces expressed astonishment and disappointment. In their eyes, being a woman completely discredited me. Never had gender slapped me in the face like it did that day.

I had to negotiate my credibility and competence to a group of men who couldn't fathom the possibility that a woman their daughters' age would be able to teach them anything about negotiation.

I tried not to squirm under their negative scrutiny. Understanding the dynamics of gender negotiation, I figured I had five minutes to demonstrate my proficiency and prove that not only was I as capable as they were, but also that I was more competent in the art and skill of negotiation than they were. They were scheduled to be with me for two days—sixteen hours! If I couldn't quickly prove that I could teach them to be better negotiators, I knew I might as well go home.

I opened with, "Gentlemen, please take a seat so I can share with you a little about my work." Then I did something I'd never do with a group of women: I bragged about myself. I knew my best course of action was to flaunt my ability as a negotiator and adapt it to how men communicate. In the world of men, bragging about oneself is second nature. It's how they prove they're competent, and they enjoy getting one up on the other.

I immediately continued with, "Gentlemen, don't let my youth and beauty fool you (humor). I've worked with thousands of executive-level professionals to teach them the art and skill of negotiation, beginning with _____," and the name-dropping began. With every high-level executive's name I mentioned, their facial expressions softened—the beginning sign of potential acceptance.

But having acceptance alone wasn't sufficient. I had to win their respect, and the best way to do that was to describe my power and status in the world of negotiation. My bragging had to go to the next level. So I began to name powerful executives I had developed in Argentina, Chile, Colombia, Paraguay, and Honduras. They became more engaged with every country I named.

Although they were impressed, I knew I couldn't stop until I'd fully convinced them that they were in good hands. That was the leverage I needed to gain their 100 percent commitment and openness to what I was there to teach them. So I continued awing them with my accomplishments, accolades, and expertise that proved I was like no other. By the time I finished, they were looking at me like I was the messiah. Fifteen minutes of bragging about myself in the most extreme way won me the respect I needed to be effective. If I tried this strategy with women, I'd be the most hated person on the planet. But the men respected me because of it.

In the end, they were very satisfied with the sessions, and I saw potential business opportunities for future partnerships. After the meetings, the men, accompanied by their wives, hosted a dinner in my honor. I knew that if I wanted to explore future business opportunities with any of these men, I had to negotiate a relationship directly with the ladies. Even deeply chauvinistic men can be influenced by their wives. Unlike negotiating with men, I'd have to earn the wives' acceptance and trust by connecting with each one of them. Some women are threatened by an attractive woman and naturally distrust her. I had to manage the impression each wife had of me so I could quickly end any insecurity or lack of trust she might have. My first step—and I needed to do this immediately so it would become part of each couple's first impression of me—was to find a positive attribute in each wife to appreciate and compliment.

As I approached the first woman, I noticed her lovely blue eyes. "You have beautiful eyes; they are absolutely stunning," I told her. Looking over at her husband, I added, "You're a lucky man to have such a beautiful wife." As I met each wife throughout the night, I used the same strategy— find a positive attribute and express appreciation for it with a compliment.

While I had already won over the men, it was important to negotiate acceptance and trust with the women as well. I've been in business long enough to know that a wife has a large amount of influence over who her husband does or doesn't do business with. I was able to successfully win them over. Some of those wives are now dear friends.

Navigating the Collision Course: Likability vs. Competence

Knowledge of the differences between how women and men approach negotiations is critical. It's crucial to understand how men think and what they respond well to during a negotiation, since it's often different from what you might do or expect. When negotiating with a man, you need to earn his acceptance by proving your competence. Keep in mind that it's important to:

1. **Establish your qualifications early on in the negotiation.** As I did with the Mexican executives, you need to impress a man you're negotiating with by using any ammo you can think of, for example, by dropping the names of influential people you both know, exploiting common interests, "bragging" about awards in your field, etc. Depending on the situation, show that you've done your homework and know your points well. Help him see you as an individual worthy of participating in the negotiation.

2. **Create the appropriate atmosphere.** Keep interactions friendly. Women who attempt to negotiate aggressively typically don't succeed. Women who do this are often labeled as difficult to work with. Many men still don't like to see their abrasive ways in a woman. They need to feel comfortable. If you challenge one head on, he will feel forced to win.

When negotiating with a man, show him that you understand the issues and are working with him on his level. Come across as a knowledgeable opponent. Boys are taught to approach the world from a competitive perspective, like playing a sport. If a man is threatened by what he perceives to be a strong woman, power issues will overshadow the negotiation. Just as some men can't handle dating a woman who is independent and confident, similar issues exist in negotiations between the sexes. Unfair? Yes! But this double standard won't change until more men get used to more women negotiating successfully.

If you try the same tactics when negotiating with a woman you'll probably put her off. Often women have different needs, as illustrated by my interactions with the Mexican executives' wives. Even today, many girls are taught to connect and play well together. (Yes, it's true: Many parents have an unconscious gender bias that is reflected in how they raise their children.[1]) As a result, girls want to make sure everybody feels good. We grow up wanting to build a friendly atmosphere and approach the world on a more personal level than boys do. Having a good relationship eases negotiations because women find it harder to negotiate with someone they don't like. Men may not care as much about liking someone, especially if the person has earned their respect. This relationship doesn't mean you have to become close friends, but it does mean you should create a good rapport between you and get to know each other a little.

When negotiating with a woman, it's good to identify some kind of common bond. But don't ever lie. Sincerity works best since, as a rule, women quickly know when they're being manipulated or patronized. If you come on too strong and don't take the time to develop a good connection, you might not seem genuine. And if you're viewed as competitive, your negotiation might get a bit rough. But if the woman you are negotiating with tries to be as tough as a man or uses a competitive negotiating style, you'll have to play her game with a similar competitive style.

Men want to know that you're credible and have earned your seat at the table. That's it. Women want to know if they can trust you. We women want everybody to get along. Men are single task–oriented and just want to know what they can get done now. They're not thinking about relationships. While they don't disregard having one, it's not their number one priority, while for women it is. We're willing to sacrifice economic benefits for relationships. There's nothing wrong with that unless you sacrifice too much too soon in a negotiation. Men perceive most situations as negotiation opportunities. We women don't. Men often focus only on the outcome and believe that relationships are a means to an end, while we sometimes think that the relationship itself is an outcome.

Leverage Gender Styles to Work Together Effectively

You can learn to recognize, understand, and leverage gender style differences. These don't make either sex right or wrong. You just need to know how to navigate them. It's important to identify the other person's negotiation style, whatever that might be, and adjust yours accordingly. The more you understand what the hot-button issues in the negotiation are and the negotiating style of your counterpart—male or female—the more successful your negotiation will be.

Pay attention to the distinct gender differences in how someone approaches a negotiation. As you recognize the person's style (more on styles in Chapter 5), adjust your technique. Use the suggestions in Chapter 1 to get comfortable in your own skin so you can build and project a positive self-image. When you *act like* you possess authority in a particular situation, it's not as difficult to have a strong position. As you get more comfortable driving a negotiation, your confidence will increase.

Some women think they need to negotiate like a man in order to be successful. No way! Our relational style lends itself more to getting to know the individual with whom we're negotiating. Developing a relationship gives you more insight into what will satisfy everyone's needs. Building a relationship is important in the growth of a long-term affiliation, so it's good for negotiations.

When men negotiate competitively, they tend to see no value in small talk and just want to get directly to the negotiation. Winning is the ultimate objective. If the other person's objectives are met, that's significant only to the extent that his needs are satisfied. Future negotiations and opportunities are considered, but the outcome of the immediate negotiation takes full priority, without concern for the relationship between the parties.

The Impact of the "Entitlement Effect" on Male/Female Negotiating Styles

Self-worth is a big factor in being a strong negotiator. Women are likely to determine theirs by what their employer will pay. Men have been taught by fathers and male peers to expect substantial remuneration for their work. This includes perks, power, personal assistants, and the like, as well as the expectation that they will earn more money than women in similar jobs over the course of their careers. Women are more likely to seek empowerment through interaction among all parties in the relationship. Men use power to achieve their own goals or to force the other party to submit. Women seek to engage, listen, and contribute. Men strive to convince the other party that their position is the correct one and use various tactics and ploys to win points during the discussion. Because these approaches are so often rewarded, they contribute to self-confidence in both sexes. None of this has to be a problem when you accept the differences, work with them, and look inside for your self-worth.

The Harvard Law School study "Women and Negotiation: Narrowing the Gender Gap" (2014) shows that negotiation skills for women are crucial to closing the gender gap in leadership.[2] Women don't have a problem developing an effective leadership style but do struggle more than men do with claiming the authority to lead. Although gender discrimination does exist, there's a behavioral factor as well. Research shows that women walk into negotiations with lower expectations than men have. There are several explanations for how our lower expectations have been conditioned.

One is derived from what's called "the entitlement effect." It's been shown that in situations where a standard hasn't been set, women tend to place a lower monetary value on their work than men do. For example, if men and women are brought into a work space, given a specific amount of money, and told, "Work until you think you've earned it," women work longer, with fewer errors. If they're told, "Work and then say how much you think you deserve," women tend to ask for less than men for comparable work.

Entitlement for economic rewards is not something women learn throughout their lives. From a young age, most girls see their mothers and grandmothers work tirelessly taking care of a family and a household for no pay. To some degree, we've subconsciously learned that we're not entitled to get paid. After all, our mothers and grandmothers didn't, so why would we expect any different? If our mothers (or we) do work outside the home, they often earn less than their husbands, and are frequently expected to make up for this "deficit" by handling a greater percentage (or perhaps all) of the unpaid household chores. The subconscious message to children is that women aren't as entitled as men to substantial remuneration for their efforts.

But when there's a known standard for how much they should earn or work, it gives women a permission of sorts to expect a certain amount of pay. When the rate is known, there's usually no difference between how much money men and women ask for, or how much they think they should work. In other words, if women know what the going rate is for X amount of work or time, they'll use that to determine what they should get. So, to increase your perceived value, you can:

1. **Build awareness.** Become aware of the entitlement effect and monitor yourself so you don't fall into the trap of expecting less than you could get.
2. **Do your homework.** *Before* you step into an interview or agree to what you'll be paid, find out what men earn for doing the same thing. Do not ask your girlfriends and use that as your standard. Women will never reach equal pay if we continue to use other women's standards for what we should expect to be paid. Instead, go to websites like glassdoor.com, which will provide you with detailed information about the differences in gender pay in certain companies and positions within those companies.

Manage Your Impression to Avoid Backlash

Having achieved significant gains in the workplace, women now face a double bind—stereotypes about acceptable behavior for women and men that are experienced in all areas of life. These double standards are pervasive in the dynamics of negotiation. Men can be considered influential and effective, even if people don't like them. As long as they're perceived as competent, they can be persuasive and get what they want. Research shows that women need to be perceived as likable by both men and women in order to get what they want. If a man behaves abrasively or uses forceful language we call him "no-nonsense," "focused," "a go-getter," "ambitious," etc., which are considered good qualities in a man. But if a woman behaves the same way or puts herself first, there can be a backlash. She may be labeled unfairly with terms like "aggressive," "selfish," and "a witch" with a capital "B."

To advance and succeed, you need to advocate for your interests, yet when you do, you may be penalized. This can make you ask for less in an effort to try to avoid making an impression that won't serve you well. Although self-promotion may be necessary to achieve your objectives, studies show that women who self-promote may be seen as violating the common gender expectation that says women are focused on others. This can adversely affect how we're perceived. (Conversely, men may risk a loss of authority and/or respect if they're perceived as overly focused on others, which is considered a feminine trait.) Negotiation requires assertive behavior, but traditional models are inconsistent with traditional female gender roles—the "nice girl" philosophy. Many women hesitate to negotiate assertively because of the backlash that can come with it, including:

- Being evaluated harshly for negotiating
- Risking less willingness to hire and work with women who negotiate compared with those who don't
- Being seen as a threat to traditional stereotypes

That's why it's important to control the image that other people have of you. Studies show that women *can* be simultaneously perceived as competent and warm if certain things are in place. While you may see this as an unfair burden, ask yourself whether fairness or effectiveness is your higher priority. A key lies in what is referred to as *impression management*. This means honing your ability to *control, monitor,* and *manage* the impression you make. How? By applying the three elements of impression management:

1. **Language:** The words you use can impress people or put them off.
2. **Tone:** The way you sound influences the impression you make.
3. **Framing:** How you convey your thoughts influences how people perceive you.

THE THREE ELEMENTS OF IMPRESSION MANAGEMENT

There are specific strategies you can use to project a likable image, which will help you get accepted by the people you negotiate with. If you adopt these into the persona you use for negotiating, you'll create an impression of yourself that will help get your points across without alienating the other person. Try using these three techniques:

1. **Use inclusive language.** Using the words "we" and "us" instead of "I" makes the person feel closer to you and subtly encourages the other negotiator to engage in problem solving.

2. **Use a strong yet pleasant tone and approach that emphasizes your warmth.** Illustrate this by showing authentic appreciation for other people.

3. **Frame the negotiation as if you were advocating on behalf of a protégé, client, or team.** Research suggests that when you act on behalf of another person or represent a collective, you'll be more effective. Have a communal motivation for asking for more. Men just need to discuss their assets. Women need to connect their competencies with a communal concern. Again, this may seem unfair, but remember your goal.

Make sure that you monitor all three elements to manage the impression you give. Stand straight with your head held high to exude confidence when you approach the people you're negotiating with. The words you use to frame your request and the tone you set for the interaction will strongly influence the ability of other negotiators to *hear* what you say more objectively. Speak in a friendly, warm, and nonthreatening tone of voice. Use "we" concepts instead of "I." For example, if you ask for a raise or for something you need, don't ask for yourself. Make it into a "we" and "us" situation: "I need to be here more hours; therefore, I need a raise because I want to be more effective for the company and can't do the additional hours without paying for additional childcare." "I'm sure we want to get this divorce agreement settled without it being too messy or depriving the children of what they need."

Whatever you negotiate for, the angle should be to benefit the person or organization. Since aggressive behavior often backfires when used by women, you'll win more when you use a softer style while still holding firm against pressure to concede "too much" or "too soon." Nonverbal behavior needs to communicate what a nice, friendly person you are. You don't have to join the boys club and become aggressive or abrasive to play to win. Using a friendly, warm, and nonthreatening tone of voice and choosing your words carefully and strategically works best. Your nonverbal behavior needs to communicate what a nice, friendly person you are but also that you mean business.

FRAME YOUR IMPRESSION USING THE SANDWICH TECHNIQUE

If the stereotype of women is warm, kind, and selfless, with the proper language and the right tone, you can frame those qualities in a winning way.

An effective way to do this is by using what's called the sandwich technique for framing·while monitoring your tone and using communal language. Like meat between two slices of bread, sandwich what you're asking for between appreciative, friendly words. Start by saying something nice to the person. Show appreciation for his accomplishments, or for how he has helped you with something. Use whatever fits the person. Then nicely state what you want and why. Then finish the sandwich by explaining how granting your request will benefit the person and the organization.

In other words, it's all about everybody else benefiting from whatever it is that you want. You should be polite and kind, but firm. Something like, "Yes, Sam. I completely see your perspective but I disagree with that." In other words, you can be very polite but assertive at the same time. Or, "We've been neighbors for many years, but since your tree broke the fence between our yards, I suggest it would be fair if you pay x percent and I pay y percent. It will be better for both of us if we can settle this privately." That's a skill that you can perfect with practice.

For example, Michelle worked as a marketing manager for a large company. Her boss, Bill, had a big ego and would call her into his office every Friday to tell her what she had done wrong that week. Michelle disliked Fridays, yet she couldn't deny that she learned quite a bit from what her boss called her Friday Coaching Sessions.

One day, Michelle heard about a senior marketing manager position open on Tom's team. Bill wasn't fond of Tom, but if she wanted to move up to senior manager on Tom's team, she'd have to get Bill's buy-in to support her move. To get Bill to support her move away from him and onto Tom's team, she decided to use the sandwich technique, encompassing tone, language, and framing.

TABLE 2.1. SANDWICH TECHNIQUE: MASTERING THE ASK

APPRECIATION	REQUEST	BENEFIT
Show appreciation	Make request	Describe direct benefit on: • Personal level • Organization level
Tie into request	Tie into benefit	Need to show how granting your request will benefit them
Thank you for spending every Friday reviewing my work and coaching me on ways to improve.	*Due to your help, I feel I have reached a new level of ability and am ready to take the next step. I would like your help in applying for an open position in Tom's department.*	*I believe that your support will allow me the opportunity to help Tom's department become more efficient and would give you the opportunity to develop new talent. Ultimately we would be supporting the organization's overall objectives of efficiency and talent development.*

As Table 2.1 illustrates:

Tone: Michelle used an appreciative tone, which sounded pleasant and friendly.

Framing: She framed the negotiation as a benefit to her boss, other employees who would have the opportunity to be developed by him, and the organization.

Language: In the benefits section she used the word "we," meaning the organization would benefit. Although she would also benefit, she did not frame her request from an "I" perspective.

Three Ways to Counter Backlash

There are strategies that can help you offset the likelihood of getting backlash for behavior that might be perceived as too aggressive or too much like a man's. You can deflect some judgments by shifting the reason for your behavior to external causes by using one or more of these techniques:

1. **Provide a situation-based explanation.** Before asserting yourself, give a good reason for why you have to do it. For example, if you need to negotiate competitively, start like this: "Larry, I don't want to negotiate competitively with you. I truly dislike it. Yet the way you're coming across tells me I have no choice but to protect myself from your tactics." You're letting him know that you're going to play hardball because "you have to," not because you want to. This protects you from being perceived as cold, harsh, or mean—nonfeminine characteristics.

2. **Appeal to external standards of fairness.** Pointing out that what you are asking for or offering is based on a standard that's set by a legitimate source implies that your competitive behavior was motivated by ethical or moral considerations. For example, if you're asking for a pay raise you can use information from professional associations, government databases, and other sources that show the normal payment for specific skills, qualifications, and positions. The use of external standards protects you because it provides a clear justification for competitive behavior. When you provide concrete information, such as referring to your skills as an asset valued by the employer, or attribute your behavior to an outside source, such as mentors who encouraged you to negotiate, you're perceived as less demanding and more likable.

3. **Show warmth and a spirit of cooperation during the negotiation.** Do this by describing your experiences working with teams and highlighting something personal, such as being a parent. If you can convince the other party that you're generally a warm person, it's harder for the opponent to blame your competitive behavior on a "pushy" disposition. However, getting the right bal-

ance of competence and warmth makes this a very tricky strategy to implement effectively. Your warmth will benefit the outcome only if it's accompanied by irrefutable proof of your competence. If it's ambiguous, your warmth may be interpreted as a lack of competence.

While it might seem impossible to overcome gender differences at first, understanding where the issues between men and women lie and finding ways to avoid the hot buttons that can trigger negative feelings can allow you to negotiate successfully with men.

Discover Your Personal Values:
Identify Your Two Most Important Principles

Refer back to the values you chose in Chapter 1 and write down your top eight values here:

1. _____
2. _____
3. _____
4. _____
5. _____
6. _____
7. _____
8. _____

Now, narrow the list to five by crossing out three of the listed values.

From those that remain, choose your top two core values.

These two value words are packed with meaning. It is likely you went through a process of "bundling"—embedding one value in another. This is not cheating; it's natural and allows you to clarify what these words mean to you.

Before your next negotiation, write down these two values and put them in your pocket. When you feel stymied or threatened, remember them and use them to guide your actions.

3

How *Not* to Sabotage Your Negotiating Power

To be a successful negotiator, a woman has to delicately combine the demanding, hard-nosed, numbers-driven male approach with the empathetic, warm, supportive female approach—and she has to do each of these things at the right time. In an article for the *European Business Review* titled "Women Leaders: The Gender Trap," authors Ginka Toegel and Jean-Louis Barsoux comment on this tightrope walk. Women have to adapt their behavior "depending on whether they are dealing upward or downward."[1] You have to be factual, strategic, and able to make hard decisions with your boss, but supportive, nurturing, and fair to employees. The following shows how a person can sabotage her own negotiating power.

Graciela Meibar, former vice president of global sales training and global diversity for Mattel, Inc., is exactly the kind of negotiator I would like you to be, and I hope you will include her among your role models. In a recent interview (and there's more from her in Chapter 18), I learned that she has not only mastered her own negotiation game, but also graciously and generously helps other women ace theirs. In our talk, she shared this with me:

"Yesterday I spoke with a young woman who is likely to get a new job offer. It means a longer commute for her, but it is a great career move. And she's afraid of asking for what she really wants in terms of salary—a 20 percent increase.

"I said, 'OK, let's do a spreadsheet. Your current commute is five miles, and to this new job, it's thirty miles. How many times a week do you fill up the gas in your car? How many more times will you now have to fill it? Let's do the math.'

"At the end, she realized 20 percent was not enough! She was going to end up losing money! Then I said, 'Now, this is just gasoline. What about wear and tear? Yes, 20 percent seems like a huge salary hike, but what is it going to cost you? Forget the emotional part of getting a promotion and a 20 percent raise; we have to look at things objectively.' She saw it then from a different perspective. I told her to go home, do the numbers, and be prepared for what to say when they make their offer."

This is a prime example of sabotaging one's own negotiating power.[2]

We've already addressed some of the cultural pressures that have sent women down less successful paths; it's now time to look at the specifics of how we act those out by sabotaging ourselves *inwardly* and *outwardly* in negotiations.

Six Ways to Combat Inward Sabotage

The most common way women give up their negotiating power is by thinking they don't have any. Even accomplished, successful professional women often doubt themselves. This leads us to self-sabotage in subtle ways, such as:

- Backing away from opportunities for no apparent reason
- Not asking for what we want or need
- Assuming others should know what we want
- Negative self-talk
- Indecision
- Procrastination
- Perfection paralysis
- Not valuing ourselves enough to charge what we're worth
- Fear of asking for more and being rejected

- Fear of not being liked or included
- Thinking small; not giving ourselves permission to think big
- Fear of overstepping bounds, making the boss angry, getting fired
- Disconnecting from your authentic self (joy, creativity, brilliant gifts) in order to "fit in"

As a result, we do not lay claim to our personal power as fully as we should or as fully as possible.

If you can honestly say you've never done any of these to yourself, then stop reading this book right now; instead, go float your resume, get a high-powered position, and give a hand up to other women who are still struggling! But if you are diminishing your negotiation effectiveness in any of these ways, you will first have to transform who you think you are inwardly in order to transform your limiting behaviors. (Unless you do this, the changes will last a few days but will disappear when you quit thinking about them.) This is my mantra: "A woman must be willing to let go of who she thinks she is in order to become who she is meant to be."

Now that you've understood the concepts, here are the actions. The six steps to inward change are:

1. **Identify.** Look at the previously listed bullet points and identify the inward processes you own.
2. **Reflect.** Think about occasions when these inward beliefs held you back. Think about what life would be like if you believed the opposite.
3. **Imagine.** Following is an imagination exercise that has helped superstar singer Beyoncé step beyond her own self-limiting self-definition. Try it for yourself.
4. **Let go.** There is nothing more powerful in the universe than deciding you are sick of thinking in a self-limiting way and absolutely have to try something new.
5. **Allow things to unfold.** Remember when you were a child and had no idea what each day had in store for you? Still, you ran outside with great expectations for play, joy, surprise, and laughter.

The Beyoncé Way

IMAGINATION EXERCISE: CREATE AN ALTER EGO

Sasha Fierce is the alter ego Beyoncé created as a tool to stretch her limits. Beyoncé used Sasha as a means to safely experiment with publicly expressing her sexuality while keeping her ladylike integrity intact. (Make no mistake: Ladylike integrity was paramount to Beyoncé's early bankability.) Sasha Fierce created limits for that very reason. Beyoncé didn't have to be Sasha Fierce; she just brought her out when necessary. No one really knew who Beyoncé was, except that she was a fabulously talented and hard-working performer with a genuinely good voice.

One way to quickly step into the game of negotiation is to do what Beyoncé did—create an alter ego. Here's how:

1. Grab your journal or a piece of paper. Write out the question, "What scares me deep to my core when I'm about to negotiate?" Allow yourself to answer, privately and truthfully. Get in touch with those moments when you're scared, uncomfortable, and just feeling less than awesome. Get them out on paper. All of them.
2. Reflect a moment on what qualities or values would counteract these fears.
3. Next, write down the answers to the following questions:
   - What superpowers would your alter ego have?
   - How would your alter ego squash your fears?
   - What would she be wearing?
   - What would her name be?
   - How does it feel to step into the power of your alter ego?
   - What phrase or code word could you use to call your alter ego into action?

Before your next negotiation, take a couple of minutes, hop into your alter ego, and show the world what you're made of.

And you got it! Step into the negotiation arena with a willingness to be open to the experiences you'll have and lessons you'll learn. How many times have I been surprised and delighted during this process? Many. You will experience these moments, too—if you grasp your negotiation opportunity as if it were a toy to be played with.

6. **Experiment.** Speaking of grasping opportunities, there will be many to experiment with in this chapter and the book as a whole. Take a deep breath, put your fears on hold, and believe you can be strong, graceful, and effective. Then—take the plunge.

The Seven-Second Rule for Combating Outward Sabotage

What you do on the inside is more important to your ultimate success, but it's what people see on the outside that produces results. Strengthening the inside strengthens the outside, so you're already halfway there. Here are some common external mistakes women make and tips on how you can up your game externally.

BODY LANGUAGE MISTAKES AND HOW TO CORRECT THEM

If a female wants to be perceived as powerful, credible, and confident, she has to be in charge of the nonverbal signals she transmits. When we act vulnerable or submissive, we diminish our authority. You may be unaware that you're doing the following, so read carefully and ask friends for feedback about whether you:

- **Physically condense.** This means taking up less room. You pull your materials into a tight pile, shove your purse far under your chair, tuck your legs under you, or pull your chair into a smaller space so your neighbor can have more room than you.
    - **My Coaching Tip:** Spread out, claim your turf, don't offer to move unless asked.
- **Nod too much.** Men nod when agreeing. Women nod when agreeing, listening to, empathizing with, or encouraging. Being a bobblehead does not express authority or power.
    - **My Coaching Tip:** Practice holding yourself like a queen. You do not have to nod. A strong neck denotes a strong personality.

Say "yes" or "okay" instead of nodding; blink, raise an eyebrow, or lift your chin *up*.

- **Wait your turn.** In negotiations, men tend to talk more than women and interrupt more frequently.
  - **My Coaching Tip:** This one actually comes from former Secretary of State Madeleine Albright, who advised up-and-coming professional women to "Learn to interrupt."[3] And don't apologize for it.
- **Are overly expressive.** Women who express the entire spectrum of emotions often overwhelm their audience (especially the males).
  - **My Coaching Tip:** To maximize your authority, minimize your movements. You don't have to keep a poker face, just a calm demeanor. Calmness plus containment equals power.
- **Allow others to limit or define you.** Your colleague introduces you in a way that downplays your role. You offer to handle an important team task, but the leader doubts that you can undertake the responsibility, even though you know you can.
  - **My Coaching Tip:** When someone introduces you in a less-than-favorable way, just add an additional comment or two to that introduction. For example, if someone were to say, "This is Yasmin Davidds; she teaches negotiation to women," I would follow by saying, "Yes, I own the only women's negotiation institute in the world."
- **Are reluctant to use politics and influence as negotiation tools.** Because politics and influence are viewed by many women as things that divide rather than unite and make people feel like excluded outsiders, the cultural pressures are high to avoid engaging in them.
  - **My Coaching Tip:** If you don't at least acknowledge office politics, you've already excluded yourself and made yourself an outsider! How is that going to help you when you negotiate with a well-connected colleague? There are good and bad politics. Good politics means building your network, which is a way of reaching out to people and creating friendships (and it's OK if friends do favors for each other on an equal basis). If

there is no way to avoid bad politics (one-upmanship, back-stabbing, damaging reputations), then at least act within the boundaries of your own personal values (be sure to do the exercise at the end of this chapter to increase your awareness of your values under pressure). You might end up setting the standard for better behavior all around.

- **Have a delicate handshake.** Weak handshakes communicate passivity and lack of confidence. (At the other end of the spectrum, and more a fault of men, crushing handshakes communicate insecurity and lack of respect.)

  - **My Coaching Tip:** Face your associate squarely and fully. Meet the person's eyes and smile; do not look at your hands. Make sure to achieve palm-to-palm contact and that the web of your hand (the skin between your thumb and first finger) touches the web of the other person's. Hold the hand firmly. A limp, fingers-only handshake isn't delicate or feminine; it's a turn-off.

You are now ready to master the Seven-Second Rule. You've likely heard the phrase "You only get one chance to make a first impression." When entering a negotiation, you must create a presence to be reckoned with, one that is respected but also puts others at ease. I call this "owning the room from the moment you walk in." *And you get seven seconds to do it.* Here's what I do:

- Get in touch with your best possible attitude of strength and confidence (or your alter ego!). Exude it through your smile and by showing genuine interest in your associates.
- Initiate a great handshake (see My Coaching Tip above).
- Continue to build rapport. Maintain positive eye contact, lean forward in your chair, smile when appropriate, and subtly mirror the other person's body postures.
- State upfront your confidence that things will end to your liking.

Once you've made your seven-second impression:

- Defuse any negativity with alignment. Sit or stand shoulder to shoulder; or turn to face the same direction as the other person if you can. If this is not possible, turn away slightly and pause to consider your response.
- Make a positive final impression. Stand tall and shake hands warmly when saying good-bye.

What You Say Can Hurt You

It's a big fear: saying the wrong thing, or saying the right thing the wrong way. It's a realistic fear, too. Women speak differently than men do because of the cultural pressures on us to be "nice" as children. Forcing yourself to speak in new ways has been known to raise very deep and real anxieties, often seeded in us by parental disapproval. Coping with these anxieties during an important negotiation is not an option; it will minimize your ability to respond strategically and creatively. This work needs to be done away from the negotiating arena, and under low-stress circumstances, until it becomes habitual.

FIVE VERBAL MISTAKES AND HOW TO CORRECT THEM

1. **Minimizing your work or position.** "Oh, I *just* manage a legal office." "I'm *only* an administrative assistant." "I'm *kind of* in charge of the information technology group." Your business needs you and thinks you're critical, or it wouldn't be paying you. Step back and identify all the reasons why your business needs you. Express pride in the ways in which you help your business reach its financial objectives, and the next time you're asked, say, "I *support* the income streams of twenty lawyers." "I *keep* the vice president on schedule and traveling with the least amount of downtime." "I'm *responsible for* maintaining my company's computers, and replacing them within budget when needed." People who speak about their current jobs in those terms are the ones who get the good job offers.

2. **Minimizing the importance or size of an achievement.** *"Just."* *"Only." "I guess." "It was really nothing." "It was luck." "For once I wasn't stupid."* Also avoid words that diminish your accomplishments or make you appear juvenile. Often, women use these words in response to a compliment. Here are some effective and strong substitutes:
   - "Thank you. I'm pleased with how it turned out."
   - "Thank you. I'm quite proud of what I've achieved."
   - "Thank you. I appreciate your kind words."
   - "Thank you. I do feel good about it. I must give some credit to those who helped me along the way."

3. **Weakening your message with qualifiers.** You say something with strength, but then become overwhelmed by a desire to backtrack because your boss frowns. Women soften their direct thoughts, opinions, and committed ideas with qualifiers to reduce situational anxiety. But these weaken your message, and your position. *"It's kind of like . . . ."* Your boss thinks, *what* is it like? *"We sort of did . . . ."* Your boss thinks what *did* you do? *"Perhaps we should . . . ."* Your boss thinks *should* we or *shouldn't* we? If you really need to soften a strong statement, do so without invalidating it. Example: "For all the reasons mentioned, I feel strongly that we should act now rather than wait. I'm curious to hear what others think." Sometimes, you may be called upon to verbalize a position about which you are not yet clear. Preface your remarks with facts about *why* you're not clear, and then explain what would make you more committed. Example: "Given the facts we have so far, I'm not sure we should move so quickly. I would need more data from Human Resources about this before making my final decision." Strong negotiators don't equivocate; they ask for what they need to move forward.

4. **Interjecting nonwords.** This is the most difficult category for most people. This, *uh,* is identifying what we do to, *ah,* present ourselves in, *uh*, an annoying and, *um*, weak way. *Right? Knowwad-Imean? Ya know? It's all good.* Only it isn't good for keeping people's

attention on your otherwise strong and salient points. One way to make yourself more aware of your verbal habits is to record yourself over the course of several phone conversations, until you forget you're recording yourself. Because no matter how diligent you are, you're probably going to be aware of only a tenth of the nonwords you actually say.

I tried this technique to good effect. I asked a close friend to coffee, and instructed her to tap the table every time I said a nonword. Woo! I had no idea! It was rough, but it gave me a whole new awareness of my verbal habits. This allowed me to effectively practice and ultimately eliminate nonwords from my professional vocabulary.

5. **Failing to pause or reflect before responding.** The art of the pregnant pause changes from group to group. The right length pause causes others to anticipate and pay attention to what you have to say. Too short, and you look too eager. Too long, and people jump in, interrupt, or steal focus. In order to prevent an associate (often male) from co-opting your turn to speak, couple your pause with a small exhale or hand gesture. The pregnant pause conveys intelligence (I'm juggling several ideas) and thoughtfulness (I want to say exactly what I mean). It exudes self-confidence (I expect to be listened to). What's the right length? Count to three, get centered on the main point you want your listeners to take away, then lead with that sentence. In some (especially contentious) groups, three seconds will be too long. Adjust accordingly.

The good news is, all this is within your power to alter. You do not have to be victimized by thoughts and behaviors that you have learned previously and continue to impose on yourself. You have the power to get out from under these burdens and make yourself heard and respected.

We all know we still face barriers; but now, we can face fewer. And that makes the ones we do face more manageable.

If you're ready to go further and practice some effective verbal subtleties, see Appendix I: Language of Negotiation.

Discover Your Personal Values:
Give Your Beliefs a Stress Test

In the last two chapters, we've concentrated on getting you in touch with your most important values. Now we're going to test them to find out how your most important values hold up during difficult times and when you must make hard choices.

Answer the following two questions:

1. *When I'm under the gun during a negotiation, what values (will I, do I) ignore?* (List some or all from the values you named in Chapter 2's exercise.)
2. *Which values got me through a tough negotiation? Which make me stick to my guns?*

4

The Four Stages of Negotiation

Negotiations do not just happen. They have definable beginnings, middles, and ends. Rather than sitting down and winging it, identify each stage so you can (1) be prepared and (2) identify the stage when shifting into it so you can respond appropriately. You really don't have to be brilliant, or even a meticulous planner, in order to prevail. You do need to understand and prepare for negotiation's four stages. These are:

1. Planning and preparation, which determines 80 percent of your success
2. Opening the negotiation; setting the tone; techniques that protect your interests
3. Idea and information exchange; moving to agreement, which includes what to do when the other side doesn't cooperate
4. Closing strategies that ensure commitment and performance

Stage 1: Planning and Preparation

Negotiation doesn't have to be a journey into the unknown. There is much you can do to prepare yourself. For starters, you need to become very clear about what you want.

Before I give you a worksheet to help you get your needs on paper, I want to take a moment to address an issue affecting many women that can hamper us as negotiators. In our roles as mothers and caregivers, we often repress our needs in order to fulfill the needs of others. If we do this too often, we lose touch with what we actually want. As a result, we go into a negotiation thinking that what we want is to please the other party.

For the purpose of the following exercise, you are to take this "want" off the table. Right now, it doesn't exist. You are to concentrate only on those things you want for *yourself* or *your business*; whether that pleases the other party or not is of no, and I mean *no*, concern. If you find this difficult, I ask you to please keep at it until you get back in touch with what you alone want.

You must have this kind of inner balance to have personal and professional fulfillment. It does not make you selfish. It makes you a strong, confident woman who is *more*, rather than less, able to fulfill the needs of others when necessary because you won't burn out neglecting your own.

Now to begin:

1. **Define the issue being negotiated.** Is it a raise? Do you want a vendor to lower its prices? Examine both your external and internal issues as thoroughly as possible. Ask yourself, "What are their initial demands?" "What do I want?" "How compatible are these desires?" "What stumbling blocks need to be removed?"
2. **Define your individual or group interests.** Ask yourself, "What do I care about?" "Why do I care?" "For what purpose do I want this?" Then rate each interest from 0 percent (least important) to 100 percent (most important—a deal maker or breaker).
3. **Define the interests of your counterpart.** Ask "What might they care or worry about?" "Why?" "For what purpose?" At first you might say, "How do I know what they want? They're going to play it close to the vest." Try an empathetic approach—what would you want in their place? Since we're all human, we can presume certain

What My Counterpart Wants

- Job security
- The esteem of their bosses and colleagues
- To be treated fairly
- To be valued as part of their team
- To feel that what they do matters
- Avoidance of risk and uncertainty
- Fun and excitement
- The sense that others (including you) like them
- To do their job well and be appreciated for it (including bringing this nego-
  tiation to a successful conclusion by their definition)
- Promotion and growth opportunities
- To control how their work is to be done
- To be free of hassle, rancor, and hard feelings
- To have their space, tools, responsibilities, budget, and rights respected

interests on their part. The box above offers some possible answers.

- If (without sacrificing your interests) you can offer to fulfill any
  of their interests, especially in surprising or unexpected ways,
  it will further the negotiation significantly. These can be helpful rewards for concessions they make to you.

4. **Select a neutral meeting site (if possible), once you know what
   you want.** Hallways and noisy cafeterias are not ideal, nor are
   large, open cubicles. Both parties suffer if talks are interrupted or
   overheard. Pick a neutral time and place to meet.

5. **Set the stage for peak confidence.** Review all of these points the
   night before the negotiations and sleep on them. In the morning,
   allow ample time to get your hair, makeup, and wardrobe just
   right. Wear whatever makes you feel like a million bucks in the
   boardroom. Looking your best breeds confidence.

Stage 2: Opening the Negotiation; Setting the Tone

In cooperative negotiation, you want your counterpart to sense their needs will be heard, considered, and respected. This encourages their more creative ideas and solutions. Certain formalities accomplish this in a business setting: (a) engaging in non-task-related talk; (b) winning them over personally ("wooing"); (c) discovering common ground, interests, and values; and (d) making verbal assurances that you wish to reach agreement.

Non-task-related talk (or small talk) is a natural activity to many women; this is how we create consensus. In a business setting, however, it's important not to get sidetracked into talking about ourselves for too long. The goal here is to learn about *them*.

We mentioned *wooing* your counterpart. Wooing works. It works because it fulfills the needs listed in the box to be liked and respected. "We're impressed with how well you've built up your business and are honored to be considered as one of your vendors." "Your reputation is very strong among people whose opinions matter most to us." It's important to be genuine, however, or you could start things off on the wrong note.

Searching for common interests. Ideally, you already will be acquainted with your negotiating partner(s) through work or social circles. If not, do some homework. Then you can say, "I understand you like . . . ," "I've heard you enjoy . . . ," "Is it true your mother is from Georgia? Mine, too." Once at the bargaining table, the desire to share personal information becomes constrained.

As soon as you sense your counterpart feels relaxed, it will be time to get under way.

Making verbal assurances. To segue into negotiating, start by assuring the other party that you've come to the table in good faith, willing to work toward fair and reasonable agreement. This is especially important if there have been prior disagreements (the last talks ended in a stalemate; the subject is divorce). "We value our relationship with you and wish to strengthen it." "We are open-minded and looking forward to hearing your position today."

Welcome them to the table formally. "On behalf of . . . I would like to welcome you . . . ." "It's my pleasure to welcome you to . . . and introduce our lead negotiator, our Vice President of Operations, Mr. Charles Smith." Then suggest a procedure or an agenda and check for agreement—"Does that seem acceptable to you? Is there anything you'd like to change?" Show respect, but don't ask for permission (it's a fine line).

If you're the lead or only negotiator, ask them what they want to achieve. "May I ask, please, what is your proposal in connection to our company?" "What in general terms are you looking for here?" Do *not* nod, interrupt, or say "Uh-huh." Silence on your part will draw out more information from them. If they look at you and wait for a response to something they've said, blink, raise your eyebrows, move your chin up, or all three.

Make only small concessions to start (and try not to be the first to do so). Every concession should serve your goal (and be rewarded). You can make a negotiation run more smoothly by making "concessions" you had always planned anyway. (Be sure to ask for things in return for these "concessions," which *they* probably had planned to do anyway. No sense leaving anything on the table!) Establishing a history of agreement at the beginning creates positive momentum.

If there are immediate negatives to handle, frequent "time-outs" or "caucuses" are your tools to assess information, upgrade defenses, and strategize new approaches. Be very generous with yourself when it comes to obtaining time to think. Refuse to allow pressure to rattle you.

Stage 3: Idea and Information Exchange; Moving to Agreement

Many women fear this part of the negotiation more than any other part of the process. They imagine they'll be bullied, duped, ripped off, or humiliated in front of colleagues and bosses for "caving in" when they should stand firm. But as you can see, if you've prepared well, the work you've already done in the previous two stages readies you for this phase. You'll be very well informed about your counterpart's desires and modus operandi, and all the verbal and nonverbal input you've received will allow your intuitive abilities to peak. If your counterpart is at all cooperative, this phase can be really fun, exhilarating, and creative.

Here are some tips for keeping things on track:

1. **Use questions to make suggestions.** Show respect for the other party's preferences, but do not ask permission. "Are we finished on that point? If so, let's go on to the next one." "Are you ready to proceed?"
2. **Plan for future impacts.** "We foresee . . . ." "We envisage . . . ." and relate these predictions to current demands.
3. **Reassure your counterparts about agreements.** You can use phrases like "I can promise you . . . ," "Have no doubts that we will . . . " to keep positive momentum building. These phrases also defuse antagonism.
4. **Clarify** any points that have just been hashed out. "So, to summarize what we heard, you're agreeable on X, Y, and Z, but not A." "Can you clarify one point for me?" "What exactly do you mean by . . . ?" "I'm not sure I fully understand . . . ."
5. **Ask "why?" and "why not?"** to ascertain your counterpart's underlying interests. "Why would you want to . . . ?" "Why couldn't you . . . ?" "Why would you object to . . . ?" "Why not try it this way?"
6. **Define** *areas of agreement* using phrases like "It involves . . . ," "It covers . . . ," "It includes . . . ," or "It leaves out . . . ."

By this point, things are coming along nicely or bogging down contentiously. If the other party is a competitive negotiator, they are proposing ways to get more and give you less. (See Appendix II: Personal and Professional Checklist for Complex Negotiations.) Competitive negotiators make demands to test how weak you are as a negotiator. There are four ways to counter this kind of pressure and show that you are a force to be reckoned with. This alone may be enough to gain cooperation and respect. Stand firm, and try the following:

1. **Ask for something in return,** such as outsourcing, personnel, budget, cost, scope of work, quality, or specifications trade-offs.

This signals that you are not a pushover. (You can learn a lot from what they say "no" to.) If you have to think fast, and nothing readily comes to mind, consider asking for more time.

2. **Ask "Would you consider . . . ?" and "What if . . . ?"** This shows that you are a problem-solver. You're willing to work with them but not cave in.

3. **Ask for their help.** This converts competition to cooperation, and puts you back onto your turf. It fulfills your counterparts' need for respect, esteem, and appreciation, often defusing competitiveness.

4. **Listen to what's underneath the words.** Make your intuition work for you to get a sense of what's really important to the other side. Take in nonverbal clues—gestures, facial expressions, as well as changes in vocal tone, posture, and gait. Are they acting aggressively because they are afraid of looking weak? Are they trying to impress their boss? Do they seem to have something important but unrevealed on the line? Try dealing with them as if *they* were afraid of *you*, instead of vice versa.

Bargaining in earnest can happen quickly, so be prepared to take control. Bigger concessions happen now—insist on rewards for making them. "We would be willing to . . . provided, of course that . . . ." "We'd be prepared to . . . ; however, there would be one condition. . . ."

This is the time to say "no." Don't be afraid to walk away if necessary. You won't have "wasted everyone's time" or get labeled "unreasonable" if you handle impasses with these five tools:

1. Making counter proposals
2. Identifying obstacles
3. Analyzing obstacles
4. Asking for concessions
5. Asking for further information

In your planning phase, you should have already decided where to hold firm. Now you may come under intense pressure to alter your position. Making a counter proposal shows the other party your intention to hold firm despite their pressure.

Identifying and analyzing obstacles validates your initial intention to make an agreement happen, while still holding firm to your goals. Often, obstacles crumble when analyzed: "We can help you achieve that, but without having to give up our position here. Let us suggest . . . ."

Now it's time to really stand up for what you want. This usually requires the other side to grant some concessions. If you come to a stalemate, ask for more information. "You said you can't do this; what's preventing you?" "You said your budget is limited to X; what about bartering additional products or services?"

Stage 4: Closing Strategies That Ensure Commitment and Performance

Closing rarely comes easily and is an achievement when it does. There are really two things required for a successful close: One is to agree on a settlement and the other is to make sure your counterpart honors it.

At this point, reiterate how your agreement will benefit everyone's interests. Stating its fairness, workability, and benefits brings you closer to the final handshake.

Objections to finalizing an agreement may surface now; it's everyone's last chance to pull a power play and force additional concessions. How do you handle this professionally?

1. Be sure you understand the objections thoroughly.
2. If there is anything you don't understand, ask for clarification.
3. Handle objections one at a time and don't generalize; this will keep your counterpart from feeling overwhelmed or defeated.
4. Empathetically resolve issues in ways that fulfill everyone's interests.
5. If you are stymied, tell the other party you believe you might have a mutually beneficial resolution, but need to think it through first. Call a time-out.

When the dust has settled, and all objections have been met, remind the other party of the benefits they will need to communicate to their company (and any internal naysayers). If further objections arise, repeat the tips above.

How do you handle deadlock? No one wants to spend two or more hours negotiating a deal only to have it end in stalemate. Nor do you want to make painful concessions. The best way is to search for a better deal for *both* parties. You can jump-start this process by asking, "On what do we agree? What are we trying to accomplish? Is there an altogether different approach we can take?" "What if . . . ?" "Help me understand . . . ."

Deadlocks need not be permanent failures. Adjourning for a day or two usually brings new perspectives. Inviting key players from both sides to an informal social event like a pizza party or a softball game may allow more relaxed discussions that lead to breakthroughs. Invite someone who has successfully confronted a similar impasse to talk about how she worked through it.

After the final handshake, unpleasant surprises can still blow up the deal. A business agreement doesn't always carry the same weight as a legal contract. For example, the person you reached the agreement with is laid off and his or her successor won't honor it. Critical materials suddenly become unavailable. Computers . . . well, don't start. But there are some things you can do to minimize the chance of a deal going dead.

WAYS TO ENSURE COMMITMENT AND PERFORMANCE

Here are some things you can do to prevent losing a deal.

- **Navigate the "reality check."** When people begin implementing their agreement, unanticipated realities may tempt them to renege on the deal. "It can't be done!" "I can't live with this agreement." "The budget is too stressed by other demands." "It can't be manufactured in three months." To tackle these impasses, get specific. Ask for details and understand the pressures your counterpart is facing. What's most challenging? When *could* this be accomplished? What section of the agreement can't you live with? How much budget is there, and how far can you get with other resources?

- **Be urgent and regular in your follow-up.** Preplan how follow-up will occur and who will do it. If there's trouble, re-involve affected players and negotiate necessary alternatives. Personnel might be reassigned; outsourcing can be considered; deadlines can be renegotiated.

- **Be on the lookout for "the nibbler."** This is the negotiator who tries to get more after the deal has closed. Nibblers are experts at exploiting unclear settlement boundaries. The *free lunch* nibble tacks on seemingly easy additional tasks, like creating an electronic version of an agreed-to printed brochure. If the free lunch nibble costs you time and money, either decline, or insist that these costs be covered.

  The *customer service/tech support* nibble imposes additional tasks on these departments in support of sales, taking up many hours that should be devoted to primary customer assistance. In your negotiations, address whether salespeople need additional training to demonstrate the product, or if additional people need to be assigned to sales support. Distribute costs equitably.

  Information technology nibbles include requests for extra testing, documentation updates, and availability for departmental meetings. Extra resources, information, and budget need to be documented and reimbursed; comp time, vacation time, and reimbursement for overtime lunches and dinners should become firm conditions.

- **Deal with "changes in circumstances."** These can be unpleasant surprises, or they can be foreseen and negotiated as part of your deal. Do your "if-then" homework. Go back to your planning stage and brainstorm possible solutions to the events listed in the box on p. 51. Be ready to craft agreeable "thens" for these "if" scenarios.

By definition, you can't anticipate the unanticipated. But you can assign certain people to put out fires. And you can have a preprepared "if-then" list to suggest alternatives. It's usually easier to incorporate solutions into an agreement just as it's about to close. Since most or all of these concerns will never occur, they become easy areas of agreement.

Handling Deal Disruptions

How do you want the following disruptions to be handled, and by whom?

- The people who made the agreement change.
- The people who were affected by the original agreement change.
- The organization, its management, or its support staff change.
- Technology and materials change.
- Needs and motivations change.
- Work specifications change in response to new needs and emerging technologies.
- Priorities change over time.
- Relations change for the worse.
- Power, influence, and authority change over time.
- Budgets and resources change.
- Economic factors change.
- Visibility into the project or participants' power changes.
- Errors and/or omissions occur.
- The worst-case scenario comes to pass.
- Something unanticipated happens.
- There is an act of God.

Armed with the techniques covered in this chapter, you'll never walk blindly into a negotiation. You'll understand what is occurring, what is about to occur, and what to do when it occurs. Practice these strategies until you know them well. You can do this in low-stress situations, for example, returning something to a store, negotiating with a friend about what activity to do or with your spouse over a small domestic matter. Think it's too much to learn? It's funny how well we remember things that bring us success.

Discover Your Personal Values: Clarify Your Definitions

Return to your original values list in Chapter 1. Write down the values that must be on your list at all times. These may be difficult choices. Next to each, define what each value means to you. Then, go back and rank them in order of their importance to you. Here are some examples:

> *Integrity:* Telling the whole truth to others and operating within the law in all business dealings.
> *Learning:* Always being open to new ways of working, no matter how well the current model is working.

VALUE NAME	VALUE DEFINITION	RANK

5

Determine Which Negotiation Style Is Right for You

We have now examined collaborative and competitive negotiation styles. There are three more. One of these five styles fits your comfort zone. The other four are tools you should acquire in case your counterpart deploys them. Being able to negotiate in different styles is like being multilingual, and just as useful in modern business.

Five Comfort Zone Styles

Before you can do this, you must first figure out what your comfort zone style is. You can do that by reading the following statements and selecting the style that best describes you:

Style 1
- I *really* dislike conflict.
- I am very sensitive to rejection.
- I am grateful for what I have and don't think I should want more.
- I am successful when others recognize me without my having to ask for or demand it; my hard work will speak for itself.

Style 2

- My primary goal is maintaining the relationship with my counterpart.
- I win people over by giving them what they want whenever I can.
- I consider the negotiation a failure if my counterpart doesn't like me when we leave the bargaining table.

Style 3

- I think splitting the difference is the most effective way to negotiate.
- I believe compromise is the fairest way to achieve an agreement.
- I believe for a negotiation to be successful, we should both win some and lose some.

Style 4

- I simply pursue my own needs when negotiating.
- I don't worry about what the other party wants; that's their job.
- I use whatever power is at my disposal to turn the tide my way.
- My main goal in any negotiation is short-term success.

Style 5

- I try to clearly define my own needs, and understand those of my counterpart, at the beginning of the negotiation.
- I aim to create mutual value and a win/win agreement.
- I am adamant that my needs be met *and* that the other side's are met, too.
- I think finding innovative solutions and creating extra value make a negotiation successful.

Which style best describes you?

If you say yes to items in some or all of the styles, you have the potential to become a master negotiator! But for now, pick the most comfortable one.

Results

Style 1: You are an *Avoider.*

Style 2: You are an *Accommodator.*

Style 3: You are a *Compromiser.*

Style 4: You are a *Competitor.*

Style 5: You are a *Collaborator.*

None of these styles is all bad or all good. They each have their uses—*and* their drawbacks. If you recognize that someone is using a certain style when negotiating with you, you immediately have extra power and leverage if you can (1) identify that style, and (2) know how to counter it if necessary. Style flexibility is one of the hallmarks of the master negotiator.

Style 1: The Avoider

Stance: I lose; you lose.

When It Makes Sense: Sadly, as a primary negotiating style, avoidance does not serve women well, although many women's comfort zones fall into this category. Avoidance, as a tactic, should be used only when you are gathering your resources to make a later show of strength. If avoidance is your natural comfort zone, you will need to practice the techniques of one or more of the other styles if you want to progress in your career.

This doesn't mean there aren't constructive uses for this style—for example, if you've been dragged into a negotiation where you feel unprepared. Or tensions are building, and you need a time-out. You can also use multiple schedule changes as a tactic to lower your counterpart's expectations. Avoidance is also a useful tactic if you are negotiating with a certain vendor and decide it's just not worth the time—after all, your time is valuable.

When It Does Not Make Sense: Avoidance does not make sense much of the time, because it will not get you what you want. Yet women often default to being Avoiders because we've been programmed to believe the following four fallacies:

1. My hard work will speak for itself, and in time people will acknowledge me for it. (*Yes. This is a fallacy. And so are the next three points.*)
2. People will think I am greedy, selfish, aggressive, and unattractive if I stick to my preferences.
3. Getting what I want is not that important.
4. I am grateful for what I have; I don't want or need more.

Here's what often happens when your primary negotiation tactic is avoidance: You don't ask for what you want (a raise, a promotion, to lead an important project, etc.). People around you assume you're not interested in these things, so they don't offer them to you. The lack of offers leads you to believe that you must not be qualified to receive them. If you're not qualified, then you don't deserve them. So why bother to ask?

Never asking/never getting is a self-fulfilling prophecy but one you can turn around, starting today. Examine the other four negotiating styles—and start using them! You will be shocked to see how much more you get.

How to Counter an Avoider:

- **Enlist allies** who can encourage or pressure the avoider to come to the bargaining table. "Your boss is my boss's best friend. My boss is thinking of talking to your boss because he wants to get this project under way."
- **Diminish the risk of saying yes.** Often when people feel pressured by too much risk, they'll avoid finalizing an agreement. Break a big commitment of money or time down into pieces or pilot projects, with payment increasing as success is achieved.
- **Make it more uncomfortable to avoid negotiating** than to come to the table. Peer, client, and executive pressure can achieve what you alone cannot.

Case Study—How to Successfully Use the Avoidance Style: Informal, preliminary merger talks have taken place between Elizabeth Corp. and Jason Corp. There are some interesting synergies, and Elizabeth has her eye on some of Jason's top talent. With a 1 p.m. meeting scheduled, Elizabeth is preparing for a collaborative negotiation. However, her morning newspapers contained articles about a Jason Corp. executive scandal that might drastically impact the value of the potential acquisition. Not wanting to shut herself off from buying the company at a reduced price and acquiring the desired talent, Elizabeth postpones the meeting for a month. For the next two weeks, she refuses to take calls from Jason Corp. executives, while she awaits the outcome of the adverse publicity. When they meet a month later, the offending executives have been fired, and Elizabeth acquires the company for 40 percent less than she was originally thinking of offering.

Style 2: The Accommodator

Stance: I lose; you win.

When It Makes Sense: Although accommodation is not an ideal stance, it can be effective if you are going into a negotiation with a weak position, because it will produce more results. It can also be effective when a critical relationship is in jeopardy, or when you or your company is at fault in some situation. If you are in a very weak position (for instance, your counterpart could put you out of business if you don't comply), graceful accommodation may be your only option. But if there is any long-term future with this counterpart, state simply and without rancor that if they take advantage of your weakness now, it could hurt the relationship in the long run. After all, trust is key for future successful negotiations, and taking advantage of you now could prove counterproductive in the future.

If you must accommodate, *try to make it temporary*. Build into the agreement that you will accommodate only for a certain period of time, or until a certain result is achieved. You may also accommodate *as a tactic to create a reciprocal obligation*. This is a good way to negotiate with your

supervisor. "Yes, Mr. Ganter, I'll be happy to accommodate your postpone-
ment of raises until after our acquisition. I'm sure you'll keep track and
make it up to me as soon as you can." You have to verbalize your needs
and expectations clearly. Accommodating without reciprocity makes you a
doormat, not a master negotiator.

When It Does Not Make Sense: In other circumstances accommodation
does not make sense as your initial approach, and it certainly should not
be your only approach. When it is, you are literally relying on the "kindness of strangers" to reciprocate your concessions. Competitive negotiators
will see you as weak and exploitable. Giving all you have upfront to gain
favor leaves you with no bargaining chips in the end. The unwritten contract of being liked in return holds no guarantee. And even if you are
liked—well liked—you will probably walk away personally dissatisfied.

How to Counter an Accommodator: There is no need to counter accom-
modators who have given you everything you want. If they've left something out or you feel there's more to be gained, you can press your demands
further.

Case Study—How to Successfully Use the Accommodation Style: At
10:30 a.m., Elizabeth's secretary announces that the mayor is on the line.
He asks her company to make a generous $100,000 donation for the city's
Fourth of July fireworks. Elizabeth's tone is friendly and open; good community relations are a high corporate priority. Although this request is 25
percent higher than last year's, Elizabeth agrees, but tells him that for her
extra generosity, she expects a great deal of media attention. She accom-
modates the request because it would have taken her longer to negotiate a
different deal, and might have hurt the goodwill she has developed with
the mayor. But she gets something in return for her accommodation: The
company receives substantial media mentions as the key sponsor, and the
mayor will undoubtedly take her calls when she needs future support.

Style 3: The Compromiser

Stance: We both win some; we both lose some.

When It Makes Sense: This style makes sense when you have a trusting relationship with your counterpart and you need to decide and act quickly. You may very well leave money, services, goods, or interests on the table, but compromising is quick and reduces relationship strain. Ideally, you will win some and lose what you can afford; nevertheless you're still losing something. This is a good default style if you have not properly prepared for the negotiation and are forced to wing it.

When It Does Not Make Sense: When you have a good understanding of everyone's interests, there is no need to compromise. Compromising sets a bad precedent and creates a stream of partial losses that might otherwise have been wins. And, although splitting the difference seems fair, it usually isn't. The biggest danger is that the party who takes the most extreme position at the outset usually winds up getting more; so, if you're the compromiser, you risk giving up more to meet in the "middle." Negotiating when you need to act quickly cheats both parties out of creating more value and discovering innovative solutions. It's a lazy option that you shouldn't take unless under pressure.

How to Counter a Compromiser:
- **Counter a blind, split-the-difference offer with a reasoned exchange:** For example, "I'd prefer a little recognition of the fact that I always pay on time and pick up my own inventory. Instead of meeting in the middle, I would argue we deserve 20 percent more than that."
- **Start with a more extreme offer than the one your counterpart offers:** "Meeting in the middle" then means you've actually gotten more than they have, while the exchange still appears fair. *Use compromise as a tactic*; later, when defending your nonnegotiables, you can point to your earlier compromise and say, "I've already stepped up to the plate. Now it's your turn."

Case Study—How to Successfully Counter the Compromiser Style: The corporate attorney calls to update Elizabeth on the slip-and-fall lawsuit filed by an employee. The attorney advises Elizabeth, "If we make our offer now, we can probably settle for less than a jury would award." Elizabeth agrees. The lawyer calls Claire, the employee's attorney, and asks Claire what her client is seeking. "We think $100,000 is fair," says Claire. Elizabeth's lawyer rolls his eyes; the employee fell in the lobby for no apparent reason. The full extent of her injuries was two bruised elbows. "We think $1,000 is generous," Elizabeth's lawyer counters. (This brings the attorney's extreme demand back to earth.) "We might think about $50,000," Claire says. "We might think about $2,500," says Elizabeth's lawyer. "I settle most of these cases for at least $25,000," says Claire. "Only when the victim lands in the hospital and misses work," Elizabeth's lawyer replies. "Neither of those things happened; $3,500 is our firm offer," he adds. "Pay $5,000 and we have a deal," says Claire. Elizabeth's lawyer counters, "$3,750 and we have a deal." "Done," says Claire. "I'll send over the final paperwork tomorrow." Where Claire has theoretically left $96,250 on the table, Elizabeth's attorney has "lost" only $2,750 by countering one extreme demand with another. The agreed-on $3,750 is well within the normal range of compensation for this type of incident, and the matter was handled within fifteen minutes.

Style 4: The Competitor

Stance: I win; you lose.

When It Makes Sense: American children—especially boys—grow up playing competitive sports, and become adults who default to negotiating competitively because they're expected to. They are rewarded by their colleagues for doing so. Among business executives who have had no formal negotiating training, you will find those who erroneously think this is the only way to negotiate. If you need immediate compliance on something nonnegotiable, then go in with competitive guns blazing. If the business relationship with your counterpart is of little concern, you can risk offending and go for short-term results. Going competitive also makes sense as a defensive tactic when your counterpart is clearly competitive.

When It Does Not Make Sense: Many women think they have to adopt this style in order to earn their place in the big leagues but find it feels awkward and uncomfortable. It definitely does not make sense in cases where you want to maintain a long-term relationship. The risk of overstepping from aggressive to offensive is very high, even for seasoned negotiators. The bottom line is that your counterpart has to lose for you to win, which is not conducive to long-term effectiveness. It's also easy to become focused on winning instead of agreeing, and deadlocks are not good business. In addition, it has the potential to damage the overall market reputation of the firm. The losers may become enemies who inflict substantial, and often untraceable, sabotage on the firm.

How to Counter the Competitive Style:
- **Use any power moves at your disposal.** "If you don't raise union salaries by 8 percent this year, I'll encourage our membership to vote for a strike." "I'm the only one with the expertise to fix this software problem in your time frame."
- **Try using *appreciative moves*.** Occasionally, these will disarm your counterpart. "We'll sweeten the deal by one quarter of a percentage point in recognition of your stellar past performance; but don't expect us to do this every time."
- **Strike back in kind.** "If you're going to require a two-week window for a two-month job, the price jumps by 300 percent." This demonstrates that you are not a pushover.
- **Ignore ultimatums.** Counter those "nonnegotiable" offers. *Name and shame the hardball tactic.* "If you think pulling this good cop/bad cop stuff on me is going to work, think again. I'll now negotiate only with the person empowered to make decisions, or else I'll report a deadlock."
- **Use humor to ease tension.** "I haven't seen this much manure spread around since I worked on my grandfather's chicken farm. Let's try retreating a little from these extremes."

- **Play better hardball than they do.** If a hardball negotiator makes a "final" offer that is unacceptable, counter with a "final" offer that is equally unacceptable. Then state that your offer is final only as long as theirs is final. For example, if Mary tells you "My last and final offer is a 3 percent discount" (unacceptable offer), you can respond by saying "If that's the case, I will purchase only 3 percent of my original order" (equally unacceptable offer).
- **Get enough other concessions to offset the loss incurred by the hardball demand.** Get agreement (in writing) on every other issue. If your counterpart's concessions add up adequately, accept some (not all) elements of the hardball demand. This is the only way to successfully handle the negotiator who values winning over agreeing.

Case Study—How to Successfully Use the Competitive Style: At 2 p.m., Elizabeth welcomes potential vendor Scott into her office. Scott wants to be the exclusive provider of plastic parts to Elizabeth Corp.'s manufacturing arm. Not happy with the current provider, Elizabeth is aware there are at least six other major vendors in the market, all of which have expressed interest in this large piece of business. Although she prefers to start off on the right foot with any vendor, Elizabeth knows that in this case an aggressive competitive approach carries little risk. She lays her demands for delivery schedule, quality control, price, and inventory management on the table; Scott tries very hard to represent the interests of his company. In the end, however, he agrees to all her demands except price. "We just cannot do it for less than $.50 per piece," he says. "I know your competitors can," counters Elizabeth. Scott calls the next day saying his company can meet her price and offers to close the deal.

Style 5: The Collaborator

Stance: Win, win; each adds new value.

When It Makes Sense: The aim of this style is to win your goals while making sure your counterpart wins theirs. It is not about compromising or accommodating. In this style, you actually get what you want, in whole; in very successful collaborations sometimes one or both parties gets more. You remain graciously adamant about having your needs met, while working to meet the other party's needs as well. The collaborative negotiation typically takes more time than other styles do, but it results in long-term client loyalty and better internal relationships. Collaboration is the preferred style in today's business environment, and most women have been trained in its ways since birth.

When It Does Not Make Sense: It is not advisable to take a collaborative approach with a competitive negotiator. Instead, make equal exchanges, "You get this if I get that." Any information or innovative ideas may be used as fodder to help the competitive negotiator win at any cost; share only after your counterpart does. Collaboration also is not an effective approach when your counterpart is not the final decision-maker, since the person's latitude to think outside the box will be limited. The collaborative negotiator facing this problem should gracefully and without rancor end the negotiation, "We have a lot to offer here that will benefit us both; would you be able to bring your president to the next negotiation session so we can begin finalizing this deal?" and build a relationship with senior counterpart executives who can fully collaborate.

How to Counter the Collaborative Style:
- **Inject reason into the needs analysis.** "I know we have a long history of successful collaboration. But we have to face facts: You've lost market share, and that brings down the value of your company's stock by X."
- **Refuse to invest time in the process.** Someone wants to do business with you, but you don't think there's a fit. Don't invest the time. Collaborative agreements are dependent upon investing time to come up with creative solutions and develop relationships; they wither when time is not available.

Case Study—How to Successfully Use the Collaborative Style: Sales are up at Elizabeth Corp. by 18 percent. However, profits are up only 9 percent. The sales manager meets with Elizabeth to negotiate a bonus schedule for the sales staff. Elizabeth feels squeezed by the per-person amount the sales manager wants because it would cut significantly into the profits and create a disappointing report for analysts who watch the company. However, Elizabeth is keenly aware of the importance of recognizing and rewarding the staff for their good results. "Dave, I can't give $20,000 bonuses; the numbers would suffer. How else might we show your staff our appreciation this year?" While Dave stalls for time, Elizabeth suggests her alternative: "How about bartering some product for European vacations for staff and spouses?" Dave lights up at the idea. "If we do that, and give $10,000 bonuses, would that incentivize your people sufficiently?" asks Elizabeth. "I'd also like to suggest allowing them to take company cars home on the weekends for their personal use," says Dave. "What would that cost?" asks Elizabeth. "They're hybrids. Our staffers would pay for personally consumed fuel; at most, I see this costing less than $1,000 per year per car for twelve cars." "I think we've got a good agreement. Congratulate your people for me," says Elizabeth. She and Dave shake hands.

Use the quick reference planner (Table 5.1) to plan your next negotiation.

TABLE 5.1 PLANNING YOUR NEXT NEGOTIATION

AVOIDER STYLE		
Behavior	**Counter**	**Use When**
Has no desire to negotiate	Enlist allies	You're not prepared
Attempts to sidestep involvement	Change the form of risk	Emotions are high
Makes power move—gains leverage, expectations	Raise the stakes for not negotiating	Not worth the effort

ACCOMMODATOR STYLE		
Behavior	**Counter**	**Use When**
Tries to win people over by giving them what they want Gives away value early; relies upon the other side's generosity to reciprocate	Accommodate strategy for now Make tactical accomodation	When you want to make deposits in the relationship bank account When you're at fault When you're in a very weak position
COMPROMISER STYLE		
Behavior	**Counter**	**Use When**
Splits the difference, incorrectly perceiving this as "fair" when used as a tactic; those who start with the most extreme position win	Use a reasoned exchange	Negotiating with someone you trust; you are pressed for time; in non-business-related negotiations; there is nothing left to offer
COMPETITIVE STYLE		
Behavior	**Counter**	**Use When**
Aggressive and unwilling to cooperate Manipulates situation in their favor Places their needs above everyone else's	Power moves Appreciative moves Ignore Use humor Strike back	Negotiating one-shot deals Immediate compliance is required Defense is required
COLLABORATIVE STYLE		
Behavior	**Counter**	**Use When**
Balances assertiveness and cooperation Assesses needs and resources to create more value Creates new value through process of negotiation	No need for counters	You need to create new value

Discover Your Negotiation Skills: Style Assessment

The purpose of this self-assessment is to help you determine your personal negotiating style.

Assessment Instructions: Read each statement in the table and record your score (0–5) in the nonshaded box according to the key below. The columns on the self-assessment correspond to one of the five negotiation behaviors. The higher your score in each area, the greater your tendency to exhibit those behaviors is. Following the assessment, you'll be able to determine where you fall and whether you need to make changes in any area.

Key: 0 = Never 1 = Rarely 2 = Sometimes 3 = Occasionally
4 = Frequently 5 = Always

HOW POSSIBLE IS IT FOR YOU TO DO EACH OF THE FOLLOWING WHEN NEGOTIATING?	A1	A2	C1	C2	C3
1. I let my hard work speak for itself; I am successful when others recognize me without my having to ask for or demand it.					
2. Maintaining my relationship with my counterpart is my primary goal.					
3. Splitting the difference is the most effective way to negotiate.					
4. I try to clearly define my own needs and understand those of my counterpart.					
5. When negotiating I simply pursue my own needs.					
6. I am very sensitive to rejection; therefore, I don't push too hard.					
7. I don't worry about what the other party wants; that's their job.					
8. I aim to create mutual value and to reach a win/win agreement.					

Statement					
9. Splitting the difference is the fairest way to achieve an agreement.	X				
10. I win people over by giving them what they want whenever I can.		X			
11. I use whatever power is at my disposal to turn the negotiation my way.				X	
12. I'll make sure that the needs of both sides are met so that both of us can come out on top.			X		
13. To win is all I strive for.				X	
14. If my counterpart doesn't like me when we leave the bargaining table, I consider the negotiation a failure.		X			
15. I push hard to get what I want, even if the other side loses.				X	
16. In successful negotiations, we should both win some and lose some.	X				
17. I like to create value in any negotiation.					X
18. I'll take the deal as is until something better comes along.			X		
19. I'm willing to invest time and energy to find innovative solutions for both parties.					X
20. I really dislike conflict.	X				
21. I usually concede first to show good faith and win over my counterpart.		X			
22. I invest the time and energy to ensure that my counterpart's needs and my needs have been met.					X
23. If I'm not prepared to negotiate, I postpone the negotiation.	X				
24. If my counterpart is willing to compromise, then I'm willing to compromise as well.			X		
25. If I concede first, my counterpart will concede as well.	X				
TOTALS					

WHAT YOUR SCORE MEANS

A1 Avoider: You dread or strongly dislike negotiating. You see the negotiating process as adversarial and find it deeply stressful. You often don't say or disclose much and usually accept the other party's first offer in order to remove yourself from the situation.

A2 Accommodator: You like to *resolve conflict* by solving the other person's problems. If the other person is also an accommodator, that person will return the favor and help solve your problems. If not, the other person takes and gives nothing in return.

C1 Compromiser: Your priority is to maintain a productive relationship. So you will *make a compromise* first, giving the other party what they want in order to reach an agreement and preserve the relationship.

C2 Competitor: You see negotiation as a game that must be won at any cost. Competitive negotiators do not give much importance to their relationship with the opposite party. A competitive negotiator believes that she has lost if the opponent gains what he or she wants.

C3 Collaborator: You want to ensure that both parties' needs are met. Collaborators expand the pie and strive to achieve an optimal agreement that maximizes everyone's needs.

6

Manage Negotiations with the "Backwards Mapping" Technique

Now you're ready to begin handling the more advanced aspects of negotiation.

"Backwards mapping" is project management for negotiation. You think about the ultimate goal first, and then go backwards, step-by-step, to see what (and/or who) it takes to accomplish it. You need to ask yourself:

- What are the right issues and ways to introduce them?
- Who are the right parties (stakeholders) to include?
- When is the right time to approach each player, and should it be done publicly or privately?
- Why should I include them, and in what order should I invite them?
- Where is the culturally ideal setting in which to meet?
- Where do we go from here if a deal doesn't happen?

The common denominator among these questions is that they should *all* be answered before the first invitation to participate goes out. This is called your *deal setup*, and the process to get you there is called *backwards mapping*.

Determine Who the Stakeholders Are

Table 6.1 is a helpful tool (and one that we'll use later in the chapter to illustrate the need for flexibility during backwards mapping of a negotiation process). It captures your need-to-know information about the critical players, or "stakeholders," in your pending negotiation.

You may not know the answers to all the questions before sitting down to negotiate. You may not even know them until an interim agreement has been reached and you've worked with your counterpart to execute it. That's OK; but if this is the situation, your strategy should be to make the shortest-term agreement possible so it can be renegotiated with better terms upon expiration when you will know all of the answers.

The following is a real-world example (with some names changed) that will help bring these concepts into better focus.

Isabella, an independent corporate trainer, was approached by ACG Corporation to negotiate a contract for her services. ACG was hired by Microsoft to recruit top-tier corporate trainers who spoke Spanish and could train Microsoft marketing managers in Latin America. Isabella was an expert in the field of marketing and Spanish was her first language. She had worked in the corporate training business for fifteen years; her standard contracts provided her with business-class airfare to Latin America on any flight over five hours, plus paid travel days. She had learned from experience that traveling coach adversely affected the quality of her training; without being compensated for travel time, the lost revenue made the unreimbursed days financially unacceptable to her busy firm.

Carrie, an ACG recruiter, contacted Isabella and asked if she was interested in a one-year Latin American training contract with Microsoft, for which she made the following "nonnegotiable" offer: "No pay for travel days or business-class airfare." In addition, the fee offered was 15 percent less than Isabella's standard minimum. On the front end, the deal did not look attractive for Isabella. However, the opportunity to get a foot in the door at Microsoft (which was difficult to accomplish) was very appealing.

Isabella knew she was sharp enough to develop a strategy to make things work in her favor, but she would not be able to do it without more information. To determine her negotiation strategy, she needed to find out

TABLE 6.1 STAKEHOLDER ANALYSIS WORKSHEET

Stake-holder name	What do I need from this person?	What are her interests, issues, or problems that relate to my objective?	How can meeting my objective help meet her interest, address her issue, or solve her problem?	How will I position my request? (framing)	When will my request take place? (sequence)

who the stakeholders were and begin her backwards mapping. There were a lot of unfilled boxes in Isabella's Stakeholder Analysis Worksheet at this point, so she took the following steps to fill them in:

1. Although Carrie proposed a one-year contract, she agreed to let Isabella sign on for only three months. This gave Isabella sufficient time to learn what she needed to know and minimize the financial impact of working for less than her minimum rate with unreimbursed travel. Carrie also told Isabella that under no condition was she to discuss contract terms directly with Microsoft. ACG had been brought in to negotiate terms with vendors; therefore, all

contract negotiations had to go through ACG. Carrie became Isabella's first stakeholder.

2. Isabella took her initial trip to Colombia, where she met Michelle, Microsoft's vice president of Latin America training. After Isabella's first training session, class participants raved about how well she did. Everyone loved Isabella and her teaching style. This earned Isabella clout to eventually pursue her requests for greater compensation.

3. That evening she had dinner with Michelle, who told her that Microsoft had been struggling for four years to find the right person to lead training in Latin America. Michelle's boss, Sandra (Microsoft's senior vice president for Latin America), was unhappy with Michelle's head count of trained marketers. Michelle told Isabella, "I think you are the perfect fit, and I'm so glad we found you. We are behind in our Latin America training, so we are going to keep you very busy this year. Welcome to the family." This clued Isabella into Microsoft's issue and gave her leverage—the scarcity of good trainers and resulting internal corporate pressure—and made Michelle Isabella's second stakeholder and Sandra her third.

4. Isabella went back to Carrie, armed with her track record and knowing Microsoft's training needs. Again, she requested business-class airfare, paid travel days, and a 15 percent increase in her daily rate. Carrie's flat-out answer came back quickly: "No."

Table 6.2 shows how Isabella deployed her Stakeholder Analysis Worksheet.

What might have been a nonproductive dead end now yields a strategy. Isabella has identified her key players: Carrie, her most difficult opponent; Sandra, the ultimate decision-maker; and Michelle, her ally at Microsoft who can influence both Carrie and Sandra. On the surface, Michelle is the person who holds the key to Isabella's success; but the contractual barrier—Isabella is not allowed to discuss contract terms with Michelle—stands in the way.

How can you get around "dead ends"? How can you mitigate having to deal with negotiators who will not negotiate?

TABLE 6.2 COMPLETED STAKEHOLDER ANALYSIS WORKSHEET

Stakeholder name	What do I need from this person?	What are her interests, issues, or problems that relate to my objective?	How can meeting my objective help meet her interest, address her issue, or solve her problem?	How will I position my request? (framing)	When will my request take place? (sequence)
Carrie, consultant recruiter, ACG Corporation	Approval of contract with 15 percent increase in fees; business-class airfare; paid travel days	Gatekeeper to Microsoft. Does not allow me direct contact to Microsoft.		Based on good reviews and Microsoft's needs	Right after first successful training session and Michelle's approval
Michelle, vice president of Latin America training for Microsoft	To direct ACG to approve my requests, or influence Sandra to do so	Responsible for Latin America development. Struggling with scarcity of good Spanish-speaking trainers. Needs the right trainer.	If she meets my demands, she will acquire a trainer who can bring Microsoft up to speed, reducing pressure on Michelle.	Without violating my agreement with ACG not to discuss terms directly	With proven track record as my three-month contract expires
Sandra, senior vice president of Microsoft Latin America	To direct Michelle/ACG to approve my requests	Latin America talent shortage. Her performance numbers depend on fulfilling talent needs.	If she meets my demands, I can fulfill Microsoft's talent needs and improve the company's performance numbers.	Cannot speak to her directly; must go through Michelle	Through Michelle as my three-month contract expires

Isabella decided to leverage her "quality of work" directly with Microsoft, in a way that would not violate the terms of her contract with ACG. Here's how she accomplished this:

1. Fulfilling her three-month contract, she conducted two additional Latin America training sessions. These earned her more respect, more accolades, and more value to Microsoft, Michelle, and Sandra.

2. At the end of her contract, Isabella told Michelle that she needed to speak to her and told her the following: "Michelle, I'm sorry, but this session may be the last training I conduct for Microsoft." Shocked and concerned, Michelle immediately asked why. "Because my three-month contract with ACG is about to end and the company is not willing to negotiate on some terms that are very important to me and that I believe are fair. ACG has made it clear that its offer is nonnegotiable."

3. Michelle said she would immediately speak to Sandra and get back to Isabella that day. Within a few hours, Michelle approached Isabella: "We don't want to lose you; we need you. I spoke to Sandra, and she said that although we cannot interfere with your current contract with ACG, we would like to bring you on board as a consultant. We will work with our legal team to ensure that we comply with our ACG contract as well." This allowed Isabella to share her concerns in a manner that did not violate her ACG agreement.

Identify the Essential Issues

In reviewing this case, Isabella's less-than-ideal short-term contract yielded valuable information and leverage. She not only learned who the key players were, but also became aware of how she alone could fulfill the desperate needs of a potentially huge client. Instead of allowing herself to be compensated at less-than-desirable levels, Isabella leveraged her superior talents into a satisfactory deal.

Isabella always kept her ultimate goals (business-class airfare, paid travel days, and her standard pay rate) uppermost in mind. These were her *right issues*; she had earned the authority to expect this level of compensation.

Mapping backwards from here, she identified the *right parties*. She developed a way to overcome Carrie's nonnegotiable stance and need for gatekeeper status; she inspired Michelle to be her ally; and she negotiated her deal with Sandra through Michelle.

Choose the Right Time

Isabella did it at the right time, after her three-month contract expired. Too soon, and she would have been passed over by ACG. While the contract was still operative, she would have incurred legal penalties. Too late, and her consulting business would have needlessly lost money.

Find the Right Approach

She used the right approach—she correctly identified Michelle as the key who could overcome both Carrie's barrier and Sandra's inaccessibility. Isabella leveraged her superior skills and obvious fit to create the need for her services; then she stood firm about the compensation she required.

Isabella also had what is referred to as "the *right no-deal options*." If it came down to it, Isabella's business would have sustained her without Microsoft as a client, paying her for her efforts at the levels she typically commanded. Therefore, she was able to walk away from the deal, whereas Microsoft, with its Latin America training pressures, was actually less able to do so.

Take the Right Steps at the Right Time

The backwards mapping that Isabella strategically employed illustrates the great importance of "sequencing" matters in negotiation. How do you determine whom to speak to first, then next? No matter how large or small your negotiation, you'll face these choices. Isabella spoke with the most difficult negotiator (Carrie) first but was able to identify the Microsoft players who could take the negotiation further along. She did not make the mistake of calling Sandra directly to tell her that she might not be able to continue to do Latin America training. She wisely worked with Michelle, whose influence on Sandra was far more substantial than her own. Backwards mapping enabled Isabella to engage her partners effectively.

The Backwards Mapping Technique

The steps that constitute backwards mapping are not always accomplished in the same order, or needed at all. Every deal is different, and unfortunately there is no magic formula to ensure success each and every time. There will be times when critical information remains hidden or you won't even be aware of the right questions to ask. Sometimes, as Isabella did, you will want to enter into a less-than-satisfactory (and short-term!) agreement in order to learn critical information that will help achieve your ultimate goal. But the following steps are solid, tried-and-true tools for negotiating your way through an imperfect, human-ruled business environment.

1. **Create a list of all parties** currently involved or who might potentially get on board, along with their interests and options if a deal isn't made. Think outside the box, but don't allow yourself to become overwhelmed. Complete your Stakeholder Analysis Worksheet and add new players as they appear. One key player can change the whole tenor of your strategy.

2. **Estimate the difficulty and costs of gaining agreement** with each party as well as the value of having that person or group on board. Strategize your way around difficult opponents, or seek to eliminate them from the process. Isabella effectively eliminated Carrie from her final negotiation by deploying both leverage and finesse.

3. **Identify key relationships.** Who influences whom? Who defers to whom? Why? Who owes something to someone? Isabella rightly concluded that Michelle was the key influencer of both of the other stakeholders, and thus was critical to her interests.

4. **Focus on the most-difficult-to-persuade player**—someone critical to the deal—and ask key questions. Find out the person's interests and desires. What will make her say yes to your terms? If you conclude that nothing will, *find out what it will take to craft the deal without that person.*

5. **Determine who you need to get on board** to maximize the chances of getting a "yes"—either your most-difficult-to-persuade counterpart or someone who can bring even greater value to the table. With Sandra on board through Michelle's influence, Isabella didn't need a "yes" from Carrie at all.

6. **Map backward** until you have found the most promising path through the forest of possibilities. Dead ends may force you to try different paths to the same place. When stymied or discouraged, don't waste energy squashing those feelings; just reorient yourself back to a logical, strategic mindset using "if-then" thinking. Don't ignore signals from your well-developed intuition, either!

Break Down Barriers

There always seem to be barriers to agreement, even when a negotiation is between only two people. Introduce more than two, and the barriers begin to compound. Some barriers can be dealt with in relatively short order; others, such as tarnished relationships, can take months or even years to break through. Confronting and managing barriers prior to negotiation is a fundamental part of backwards mapping. Plan for them; then plan around them.

Sometimes, a barrier is just that last-minute gut feeling that something simply isn't right. You might not have words to define it, even to yourself. Does it originate from you, or is it coming from them? Giving barriers a name will bring them into focus.

Following are some common barriers and the opportunities they present to the well-prepared negotiator:

BARRIER	OPPORTUNITY
Issues Barriers	
The agenda is too narrow.	Broaden the agenda; think outside the box.
The agenda is too broad.	Break it into pieces, possibly involving multiple agreements.
People Barriers	
Relationships are tarnished.	Change contact people; mend relationship; make building productive relationships a management priority.
Wrong people are at the table.	Invite potential allies; exclude or neutralize adversaries with allies.
Too many people are at the table.	Exclude all but the most powerful/ influential.
Rules Barriers	
There are historical, social, or cultural rules.	Master the rules. Know how and when to use them as well as when to break them.
Legal constraints exist.	Change the rules by lobbying lawmakers.
Interests Barriers	
Opposing positions are deadlocked.	Find greater value for both sides and enlarge the pie.

One of the decisions you must make when undertaking backwards mapping is whether to approach potential players publicly or privately. How much of your negotiation should be open and inclusive? How much should be closed and exclusive? You may be able to come to an agreement quickly in an open meeting with people you know well, but you might also be tipping your plans to a secret enemy. James K. Sebenius, Gordon Donaldson Professor of Business Administration at Harvard Business School and a member of the Executive Committee of the Program on Negotiation at Harvard Law School, warns: "Relying on inclusive meetings can be risky. Interests and agendas may surface that are better dealt with privately in a careful order. Large, open meetings may help opponents to identify each other, meet, join forces, and thus mount a more powerful combined challenge."[1]

Here are just a few questions to ask yourself that will provide topics for private discussions prior to coming to the table:

- Will you save money if you negotiate with certain buyers or sellers privately prior to coming to the table?
- If you get several key people in agreement first, will this coalition be able to beat back any anticipated opposition?
- If you get one person to say yes, will that convince another to become an ally as well?

If you don't first backwards map to plan and implement these activities, you may doom your negotiation to substantial delays, even failure.

As you can see, one of the secrets of master negotiators is doing the bulk of the work before negotiations ever open. They know to whom they're talking, what their opponents care about, and who has the power to sign off. They've taken steps to allay opposition. While master negotiators may be eloquent and quick thinking, they don't rely solely on these abilities to get the deal done. And neither should you.

Master negotiator and former U.S. trade representative Charlene Barshefsky has negotiated with hundreds of governmental and private entities. Her advice: "Tactics at the table are only the cleanup work. Many people mistake tactics for the underlying substance and the relentless efforts away from the table that are needed to set up the most promising possible situation once you face your counterpart."[2]

Do your homework—always backwards map first.

Discover Your Negotiation Skills: Backwards Mapping

Start practicing for your next negotiation using the backwards mapping worksheet below. Think of an upcoming negotiation and go for it! If none is on the horizon, consider a previous negotiation; how would doing this exercise have improved the process?

BACKWARDS MAPPING

1. Create a list of all parties involved in negotiation using your Stakeholder Analysis Worksheet.	*List all of the parties involved.*
2. Estimate the difficulty and costs of gaining agreement with each party. Who will be most difficult to get on board?	*What is the difficulty and what are the costs of gaining agreement from each party?*
3. Identify key relationships.	*Who influences whom?* *Who defers to whom? Why?* *Who owes something to someone?*

4. Focus on the most-difficult-to-persuade stakeholder—someone critical to the deal—and ask key questions.	*How can I gain buy-in from my most-difficult-to-persuade stakeholder?* *What are the person's interests and desires?* *What will make him or her say yes to your terms?*
5. **Determine who you need to get on board to maximize the chances of getting to "yes"** (either your most-difficult-to-persuade stakeholder or someone who can bring even greater value to the table).	*Who can I bring on board who will give me leverage?* *How can I leverage that person's buy-in?*

PART TWO

BUILD LEVERAGE WITH YOUR NEGOTIATION TOOLBOX

You are surrendering power if you:

1. Allow disrespect in your life to satisfy your need for approval and "love"
2. Allow someone to speak to you in a derogatory or degrading way
3. Don't speak up when you should
4. Are not your authentic self
5. Stay in situations that are not good for you
6. Say yes when you want to say no
7. Agree with people you know are wrong
8. Allow negative influences to invade your mind and sap your energy
9. Live life on life's terms *instead of your own terms*

7

Offensive Maneuvers and
How to Counter Them

This is your introduction to playing in the big leagues, and I suggest you take a lot of time with this chapter. It will familiarize you with all the most important offensive maneuvers and their countermoves. Watch how these tactics unfold in your daily life; they'll pop up in even small interactions. Once you've identified and successfully countered them a few times, they will be ingrained and you will not have to memorize them. Just choose one a day, or one a week, and work with it until you've had some experience successfully deflecting it.

To become a master negotiator, it is imperative to wake up to the tactics of masters and respond appropriately. Create your own level playing field; know that for every tactic there is a countertactic or defense. It is important to note that I am *not* suggesting that you get in there and skirmish proactively. That's because women experience lesser outcomes and backlash when they play hardball. They are, however, rewarded with respect when they are able to masterfully deflect hardball tactics.

Many cultures make women the repositories and protectors of better, more gracious behavior. Australian behavioral researchers Carol Kulik and Mara Olekalns have shown that employing hardball tactics *lessens* a woman's chances of success in negotiations because they appear to be taking the low road; men who act like women by fostering relationships, listening, and collaborating increase their chances of success because they appear to be taking the high road.[1] The way we women negotiate is actually more successful for both men *and* women! So why backslide?

Defend Yourself Against Hardball Tactics

That said, a good defense is the best offense. Here's how to deflect hardballs that are thrown in your direction:

Tactic: Deferring to Higher Authority Offense: The other party claims they can negotiate only on certain items, while other terms are nonnegotiable and fixed by a higher authority; or final approval can be given by only that person.

Commonly Used By: Car salesperson, who keeps running to the boss while you cool your heels; counterparts who "must get approval" from a boss or a board.

Defense:
- Make certain you understand why you are not dealing with the ultimate decision-maker *before* you sit down to the negotiating table. It may make sense to refuse to negotiate with anyone other than that person, and to reschedule the meeting if that person is not present. In other situations, creating a positive relationship with the lower-level person can shift the ultimate outcome in your favor if you create an ally. A vice president who goes to bat for you with the CEO can help win board approval.
- If you are not negotiating with the ultimate decision-maker, do not accept nonnegotiable terms as nonnegotiable. If you do, you will be hit with more and more of them. *Nothing* is nonnegotiable (except your values)! Unearth the interests behind these items; find out why they're nonnegotiable, then insist on access to the higher authority to renegotiate a *mutually* favorable outcome. If you are negotiating

with the highest authorities, call them on this tactic and politely encourage them to do their job as decision-makers.

Tactic: Name-Dropping Offense: Your counterpart may mention having done business with a VIP or an esteemed company, or having interacted with famous personalities.

Commonly Used By: Vendors who want to do business with your firm; consultants trying to impress (or override) you.

Defense: It is human nature to be awed by fame and celebrity. Recognize what is happening and do not allow yourself to be starstruck or overwhelmed.

- Consider how you would treat the vendors or consultants if they did not have these associations. Is there some reason to treat them differently because they have connections?
- And how do you know for sure that they have these associations? Before you accept these assertions, make detailed inquiries about the exact nature of the association. If your counterpart is vague, disregard the claims. If legitimate, negotiate an introduction. The addition of celebrities and powerful people to your network provides the potential for valuable future access.

Tactic: The Set-Aside Offense: During the negotiation, the other party may attempt to avoid addressing certain issues due to an unwillingness or inability to satisfy them, or may raise issues to throw you off track. They don't want to appear to be saying no, but they won't revisit these issues.

Commonly Used By: Government committees struggling with political pressures; vendors that have cash flow, staffing, or union problems; companies that know they're going to be acquired or merged but can't discuss the situation and need to remain flexible and avoid new obligations.

Defense: Your negotiation preparation will reveal at least some of what your counterpart's main interests are. Using these interests, redirect the discussion back to those avoided issues and propose collaborative solutions. Never let a set-aside issue become a permanent "no" if it's not in your best interests.

Tactic: Precedents Offense: A previous decision or outcome may be used as a guide or justification for a similar course of action. Precedents can be useful, but they sometimes hinder or prevent needed growth, change, and creative solutions.

Commonly Used By: Lawyers who are bound by legal precedents; bosses who have organizational precedents, such as marketing departments that resist changes to corporate logos or colors; and administrators who resist streamlining existing procedures.

Defense: Precedents should usually be accepted; otherwise, you erode your own credibility. If you need to take a time-out to research the validity of a precedent, take it. Not all precedents are valid, documented, interpreted, or even remembered correctly. A good defense against precedents is not to set any early in the negotiation.

Tactic: Good Cop/Bad Cop Offense: Usually (but not always) played with two or more counterparts, one demanding concessions while the other seems more reasonable. Note: This game can be played on you even if there is only one other negotiator—the counterpart "wants" to collaborate but continually refers back to a constraining party. Remember the line, "Wait 'til your father gets home"?

Commonly Used By: Judging from police procedurals, it's a common police tactic used to get a suspect to confess (sadly, many parents do this trying to convince a recalcitrant child to do something he doesn't wish to do); any counterpart (corporate lawyers, firms with which you want to do business) who believes the combination of threatening and cajoling you will wear you down.

Defense:
- Focus on your own interests. It is critical to understand that although the good cop appears to be on your side, she really isn't.
- Don't ask the good cop to intercede on your behalf; this gives away your power.
- Commenting on the tactic (especially with humor) often disarms it: "I feel like I'm in the interrogation room on a cop show! You wouldn't intentionally do that, would you? Let's get back to the reason why we're here."
- If humor is ineffective, concentrate all your efforts on the bad cop; discover and address his or her concerns.

Tactic: Delay and Stall Offense: Holding negotiations up in an effort to wear you out and compel you either to capitulate or be more flexible.

Commonly Used By: Both sides during union negotiations, or any negotiation where there is a deadline that creates pressure as well as any vendor or acquiring firm that knows you'll lose money if you have to wait.

Defense:
- Be aware that the purpose of this is to wear you out so you give in or become more flexible in your demands. If there is a deadline involved that puts you under pressure, it probably pressures the other side, too.
- Remain emotionally detached and resist imposed deadlines. (Most deadlines are negotiable anyway.)
- Tell the other party that you know what they're doing and why, and it will not work—this is surprisingly effective.

Note: If *you* have a deadline, try not to communicate it, but set a deadline for the other party that is well within your time frame.

Tactic: Extreme Claims Followed by Slow Concessions Offense: This is used by counterparts who believe they hold more power and are going to squeeze the most out of you.

Commonly Used By: Attorneys in divorce proceedings, where one spouse has been proven adulterous; real estate agents in sellers' markets; parties who are suing you; bosses who have several good candidates for a position.

Defense:
- Exhibit any natural flinch response or show surprise.
- Even laughing at the offer is OK. Laughter can defuse tension and facilitate deal making.
- Cite other deals as precedents and tell your counterparts you expect them to adjust their expectations and make a more reasonable offer.

If all you do is make an extreme counterproposal, you run the risk of meeting in the "middle" in a situation where the middle is not advantageous to you.

Tactic: Take-It-or-Leave-It Offense: A "final" offer is made at a premature stage in the negotiation from a position at the outer edge of a possible zone of agreement.

Commonly Used By: Salesperson who has sensed your interest or desire for the item—most often when the negotiation is for a high-priced commodity like houses, cars, furniture, antiques, or appliances; a boss who has several good candidates he or she could hire; a company with a choice of several good vendors or consultants for a project; anyone involved in negotiations involving high monetary stakes as a gambit to test the strength of the other party.

Defense:
- If this tactic is employed relatively early in the negotiation, it is usually a bluff; you'll need to call your counterpart out. "If I were to agree to this demand, would you be prepared to sign an agreement here and now?" This does not commit you, but flushes out the other party's tactic.

- If it happens in the middle of the negotiation, counter to get something back for accepting the demand; don't give in without a commensurate reward.
- If it happens at the end of a negotiation, it may signal extreme frustration and a desire to walk away rather than continue negotiating. This must be handled with care. Can you walk away? Can you come back to the table if you do? Can you collaborate and think outside the box to achieve another desirable outcome? "I can neither take nor leave this offer. I would like some time to think through how we can both get what we want, as I am out of ideas today."

Tactic: Personal Insults and Feather-Ruffling Offense: Your counterpart makes matters personal to get you rattled. He senses that you operate emotionally and will try to turn that into a weakness he can exploit, rather than focus on the issues.

Commonly Used By: Male negotiators against females (most frequently employed against younger or newly hired women to gain the upper hand by destroying confidence); also used against negotiators from companies recently involved in scandals.

Defense: Don't give your counterparts the emotional response they want. Refuse to be thrown off balance or to acquiesce. Smile at them, as if amused by their childishness. Calmly and confidently remind them that such tactics (and you're aware that this is what they are) are unprofessional and that you are there to negotiate dispassionately about issues, not people.

Tactic: False Anger or Show of Temper Offense: Another tactic that attempts to turn your emotions against you by threatening irrational aggression. It is designed to create uncertainty or fear.

Commonly Used By: Attorneys in divorce proceedings and in actions against counterparts who prioritize customer service or maintaining long-term business relationships.

Defense: Same as personal insults defense above.

Note: If extreme anger or real rage occurs, leave the negotiation as quickly and safely as you can, and do not reengage except through an intermediary. Do not worry about making the wrong call between false and real anger; trust your instincts.

Tactic: Preconditions Offense: They refuse to negotiate unless you make big concessions upfront or give them the information they demand, without offering anything in exchange.

Commonly Used By: Both sides during union negotiations; strong negotiators against perceived weaker negotiators; companies about to make a big purchase from a vendor.

Defense: You're either at the bargaining table, or you're not. If preconditions are insisted upon "before we sit down to negotiate," you're already negotiating, and don't let them make you think otherwise. All the standard negotiation tactics apply, including asking for concessions in exchange for their "preconditions."

Tactic: Agreement . . . "If" Offense: A false agreement that comes with a series of conditions or potentially unfulfillable contingencies.

Commonly Used By: Females against male negotiators.

Defense: It is sometimes difficult to determine whether an agreement is false. It will look like an actual agreement, until the demands for extra concessions start piling up. Understand that there really is no agreement in place, and you will not lose anything by continuing to negotiate item by item. "So we really weren't even close to an agreement, were we?" is one way to disarm a deal that seems close, but isn't.

Defensive Tactics for All Occasions

So far, I've covered actual tactics and specific defenses that you can use to deter them. There are also broader defensive tactics that can be applied in a variety of situations. Here is a real-world example (with names changed) that will demonstrate their efficacy.

Divina was a high-level attorney for a top film company. A client hired her to represent his interests in a third-party negotiation against one of the leading negotiation companies in the country, DXY Corporation. Because planning is 80 percent of negotiation success (see the bulleted list that begins the discussion of backwards mapping in Chapter 6), Divina did her homework.

Her first step was to *gain clarity on her objective*—what she was attempting to accomplish through the negotiation. Her second step was to *gather intelligence*—information is power. Information gives you options and suggests the most effective strategies. Her first priority was to *create a negotiator profile* of the opposing lead player:

- She *researched the individual and organization*. Note: If the negotiation had involved international counterparts, she would have *researched the country's culture and politics* as well.
- She *talked to people about her counterpart's history and behaviors*. From this, she *anticipated his likely negotiation style* and *planned her own*.
- She *attempted to list all known objectives, interests, priorities, and goals of the other party*. These included financial, political, reputational, moral, aspirational, and any other details, which helped her to *plan her list of desired concessions*.

To start her negotiator profile, Divina called in a favor from a colleague at DXY Corporation, Carol Delano. "Carol, can you check your system and tell me who is scheduled to negotiate the ABC deal?"

"Jim Calderon," replied Carol.

Divina's heart dropped. Jim Calderon had been in the business for twenty-five years, and had a reputation for being relentless. He was a master at the game of competitive negotiation, brilliantly using power tactics to gain leverage. In comparison, Divina, despite her many years' experience, was a novice. But she knew that the perception of power was more important than real power; she also knew pressures on DXY had brought the company to the table, so she had a slight advantage.

Carol continued. "A team of six other negotiators is scheduled to join him."

"Carol, that must be a mistake! This was supposed to be a one-on-one negotiation, not a team play. I can't possibly gather a team by tomorrow morning." Divina thanked Carol, hung up, closed and locked her office door, and sank into despair.

Negotiation Is About Perception, Not Reality

Divina had faced power tactics before. Fortunately, this time she had warning. In competitive negotiations, power continuously shifts based on new information and new or stalling tactics. Jim was using an intimidation tactic called power by numbers, surprising her with a team of six. She needed to change the game. It was clear she couldn't create the perception of power if she was forced to take on all seven negotiators alone.

POWER POSING AND PERCEPTION OF POWER

In every negotiation, power is the element that ultimately gives the advantage to one party over the other. Tactics are used to increase one's own power, or decrease the power of the other. Jim had moved to decrease Divina's power. She retained her power through thorough preparation, and now she was about to deploy it.

NEUTRALIZE PRENEGOTIATION POWER PLAYS

Perception becomes reality. Divina needed to counter Jim's "power by numbers" tactic by walking into the room the next morning with what Jim perceived to be a team of six additional negotiators of her own. Her Rolodex yielded six colleagues who knew nothing about negotiating or the contract under consideration but were up for a challenge. She called each of them and said, "Put on your best suit and meet me at the blue towers tomorrow at 9 a.m." Divina then briefed her team actors on how to create a perception of power: "When our opponents walk into the conference room, do the following:

"Avoid eye contact with the opposing team." This gives the illusion that Divina's people cannot be trusted, creating uncertainty in her opponents.

"Do not smile; keep a straight, serious face." This minimizes expectations of friendliness and emotional exploitability.

"Do not say a word." Make the opposing team break the uncomfortable silence.

"Every twenty minutes, call a caucus (a short break)." This creates the illusion that you are strategizing.

These tactics, Divina hoped, would shield her from having to reveal the shortcomings of her fake negotiation team.

DEFINE THE NEGOTIATION PARAMETERS

Whether you are weak or strong going into a negotiation, there are many ways to grab power. One is to set the rules of the game. Divina changed the structure of the negotiation in every way she knew how. She couldn't alter the timing or sequence of the agenda. The date and location in a neutral setting were already confirmed. Because Jim had changed the basic rules of the negotiation from one-on-one to team, Divina changed the rules yet again by assembling her own team. She also took control by calling time-outs for her own purposes and used this tactic to good effect.

SET THE SCENE

Even if the location is beyond your control, its use can still be within your power to dictate. Divina instructed her team to be the first ones to arrive in order to set up the space, and thereby spread out and claim ownership. She instructed her team to sit with their backs to the window. This would force the other team to look into the light, silhouetting Divina's team and making their expressions harder to read. Her team also would not be distracted by the view.

She had her team members adjust their chairs as high as they could go, giving them a slight *height advantage* relative to the opposing team and thereby ensuring that this intimidation trick would not be played against her.

MANAGE TACTICS AT THE TABLE

When Jim and his team entered a half hour later, they were shocked to see Divina and her team seated in the power positions with their backs to the windows. "Interesting seating arrangements," sneered Jim, employing a credibility trashing tactic.

"Interesting situations call for interesting seating arrangements," replied Divina with a smile. In response to Jim's subtle attack on her ethical standards and motives, Divina's reply functioned as a *credibility cleaner* and *legitimized her motives*. It was important that Jim's team saw her as fair and ethical.

As instructed, Divina's team periodically glanced over at the negotiators on the other side, yet never allowed their eyes to meet. They pretended to be taking continuous notes as the other side made their points. Every twenty minutes, one of Divina's team members called a caucus to discuss the ongoing negotiation. At least that's what she led Jim's team to believe; they really just huddled and pretended to discuss strategy.

All these caucuses made Jim's team nervous as they tried to determine their strategy and adjust their tactics. After six hours, they came to a mutually beneficial agreement.

As Divina was leaving, Jim stopped her and said, "I just want to tell you how impressed I was by you and your team. It took us a while to figure you out."

Divina's heart raced. Was he going to blow her team's cover?

"You had us fooled at first, especially when no one on your team but you spoke, and all those caucuses were making us nervous until we figured out you had a team of body-language experts reporting back to you every twenty minutes so you could plan your next move. Nicely played."

Divina never revealed the truth of her ploy to Jim.

The Role of Experts in a Negotiation

Divina built an effective backup team of people who didn't have any negotiation skills or background in the particular issues at hand. Imagine how much better you can do if you assemble a team of people with real expertise or skills.

Experts are always a good choice. Depending on circumstances, you might consider inviting internal or external experts who can bring financial, economic, marketing, mathematical, engineering, or scientific information to the table. Unless your counterpart invites an expert of equal or greater caliber, the information your expert provides gives you a distinct advantage, without calling your feminine warmth or likability into question.

The same is true for *authorities*. Legal, governmental, and regulatory authorities are hard to dispute.

Never underestimate the power of surrounding yourself with *allies, friends, or family*. Members of family-owned businesses, especially, make very strong negotiators because they have each other's backs with firmly shared interests. Your allies and friends have the power to help you stand firm—you don't want to have to face them tomorrow if you cave in!

There are other, more esoteric tactics that may be used against you, and we will touch on most of those in future chapters. Right now, start to recognize when these tactics are being used on you in everyday life (you may be surprised who's doing it). Then counter in one or more of the ways described above. Claim your power and own your game. Remember:

There are only two options in the game of competitive negotiation:
Play. Or be played.

Discover Your Negotiation Skills:
Name the Tactic

Before you can counter your counterpart's tactics, you must be able to identify them. In the table below, Column B describes a particular tactic; Column C names the tactics covered in this chapter. In column A, put the letter of the tactic described in Column B. See example below.

NAME THE TACTIC	DESCRIPTION OF TACTIC	TACTIC NAME
Column A	Column B	Column C
1. __H__	Usually (but not always) played with two or more counterparts, one demanding concessions while the other seems more reasonable.	A. Precedents B. Name-dropping C. Preconditions D. Set-aside
2. _____	The other party claims they can negotiate only on certain items, while other terms are nonnegotiable and fixed by a higher authority; or final approval can be given by only that person.	E. Extreme claims followed by slow concessions F. Personal insults and feather ruffling
3. _____	Another tactic that attempts to turn your emotions against you by threatening irrational aggression. It is designed to create uncertainty or fear.	G. Defers to higher authority H. Good cop/bad cop
4. _____	Holding negotiations up in an effort to wear you out and compel you either to capitulate or be more flexible.	I. Take-it-or-leave-it J. False anger
5. _____	A "final" offer is made at a premature stage in the negotiation from a position at the outer edge of a possible zone of agreement.	K. Delay and stall
6. _____	A previous decision or outcome may be used as a guide or justification for a similar course of action.	

7. _____	During negotiation, the other party may attempt to avoid addressing certain issues due to an unwillingness or inability to satisfy them, or may raise issues to throw you off track. They don't want to appear to be saying no, but they won't revisit these issues.	
8. _____	Your counterpart may mention having done business with a VIP or an esteemed company, or having interacted with famous personalities.	
9. _____	This is used by counterparts who believe they hold more power and are going to squeeze the most out of you.	
10. _____	Your counterparts make matters personal to get you rattled. They sense you operate emotionally and will try to turn that into a weakness they can exploit, rather than focus on the issues.	
11. _____	They refuse to negotiate unless you make big concessions upfront or give them the information they demand, without offering anything in exchange.	

Answers

2. G   3. J   4. K   5. I   6. A   7. D   8. B   9. E   10. F   11. C

8

Power Moves for Handling Difficult People

In this chapter, I want to open a window onto a world where difficult people don't exist. They may appear difficult when you encounter them, but being hard to deal with is not really who they are inside. It will help if you think of every person with whom you do business in this way.

People *become* difficult because they think these behaviors will get them what they want, or prevent what they don't want from happening. Surprisingly, there are only three types of difficult people. (There are people whose difficult behavior is the result of mental illness or addiction. Such behavior is not a choice. In such cases, alert your supervisor or Human Resources Department.) And there are just four techniques for handling them! Not so hard. Your goal: Bring them to their senses, not to their knees.

So what makes these three types of people difficult? Read on.

1. **The Intentionally Difficult Person.** Such negotiators make a strategic, behavioral, or philosophical choice to come on strong. They criticize you, wear you down, and try to break your confidence. This technique has a proven track record of getting these negotiators what they want.

2. **The Accidentally Difficult Person.** Such negotiators have good intentions but lack the skills to create a win-win. They issue orders rather than craft solutions and force obedience rather than inspire buy-in. At the same time, they don't seem comfortable acting this way. They lack collaborative bargaining role models.

3. **The Unfulfilled Difficult Person.** These negotiators feel that their needs are not being met. They will stonewall, delay, and deny until those needs are recognized. They themselves may not understand those needs (or may not think it's a good idea to tell you about them).

We've all met people like the three types above. We may work for one, or even have been one ourselves. We all get forced into corners, are pressured by others' expectations, or are left wanting upon occasion. Understand that beneath the surface of a difficult person lies someone who just wants his or her needs acknowledged.

Here are the four power moves you can use to make this happen:

1. Diagnose—don't react
2. Disarm—consider their perspective and show them you're on their side
3. Reframe—change the game
4. Build a "golden bridge"—make it easy to say yes

Here's how these moves work with each type of difficult person.

Dealing with the Intentionally Difficult Person

Intentionally difficult people are the archetype of the hard-driving negotiator. Their experience has "proven" that hard bargaining is the most effective strategy. Early on, they may attempt to manipulate you with displays of anger. They're testing your breaking point; manipulative negotiators who use anger as a tool (they're probably not angry at all) are quite effective at gaining concessions. Research by Kristina A. Diekmann of the University of Utah, Ann E. Tenbrunsel of Notre Dame University, and Adam Galinsky of Northwestern University shows this tendency to back down is typical of human behavior, despite our best resolve.[1]

POWER MOVES WHEN NEGOTIATING WITH INTENTIONALLY DIFFICULT PEOPLE

When negotiating with an intentionally difficult person, your collaborative behavior will be treated as weakness. Instead of collaborating, use the four power moves in the following ways:

1. **Diagnose—don't react.** Call the person on it or simply ignore her tactics.

   Vanessa (Employee): Ms. Gomez, may I talk to you for a moment?
   Ms. Gomez (Boss): If it's about a raise, Vanessa, I'm afraid the answer is no!
   Vanessa: But I haven't even asked you yet.
   Ms. Gomez: Don't ask. There's no money in the budget. Period.
   Vanessa: But it's been two years since my last raise.
   Ms. Gomez: Did you hear what I just said? There's no money in the budget. I thought I made myself perfectly clear!

   An angry response from Vanessa at this point could destroy her career's upward momentum. Instead, she takes an emotional break (sometimes called "going to the balcony") to remember her main interest is to get the raise and maintain a working relationship with the difficult boss.

2. **Disarm—consider their perspective and show them you're on their side.** To disarm intentionally difficult people, act as their equals. Do what they do; throw their tactics back at them. Rather than making the situation worse, you'll often gain their respect and find they back off—even if only a little. Make an angry show of your own (after explaining you don't normally like to negotiate this way but they've backed you into a corner). Show them you

won't be bullied. Use pressure tactics that lead them to realize the status quo is unacceptable.

Once you've convinced them you're a strong equal, communicate agreement to them on every point on which you genuinely agree. This can be very disarming and cause them to treat you as they would any good friend. Another disarming tactic is to see the world through their eyes.

Vanessa (Employee): I realize we have a very tight budget; I wouldn't ask you to blow the budget to give me a raise.

Ms. Gomez (Boss): You wouldn't?

Vanessa: No, of course not. The last thing I want to do is put you on the spot.

Ms. Gomez: Then what do you want to talk about?

Vanessa: I would like to discuss how you think I'm doing overall, what I can do better, and what I can expect in return—knowing there's no money in the budget.

Ms. Gomez: We can talk at 1 p.m. but, remember, a raise is not an option.

3. **Reframe—change the game.** Change the negotiation to problem-solving. Ask difficult people how it might be handled. Give them choices; ask them their preferences and reasons for certain demands. Why do they behave so aggressively? What do they stand to lose or gain? How can you give them what they really want and fulfill your needs at the same time?

Vanessa (Employee): I've been thinking about the tight budget we are operating under. Is there any way I could help us save money by taking on additional responsibilities?

Ms. Gomez (Boss): Well, that's an interesting question. Let's see now . . . .

4. **Build a golden bridge—make it easy to say yes.** When facing an aggressive adversary, it's always good to bring backup. Enlist allies

who will encourage the intentionally difficult person to negotiate collaboratively rather than competitively. Invite people your opponent respects, for example, lawyers, doctors, scientists, supervisors, government officials, friends, celebrities, or someone who wants to hire you away. These people may actually be present or they may provide something in writing.

Vanessa (Employee): I realize a raise right now is impossible. But *if* I'm able to help us cut costs, could you compensate me out of the savings that result from the extra tasks I'll be undertaking?
Ms. Gomez (Boss): I'm not sure any of this will actually work. I can't blow the budget on the basis of your promises.
Vanessa: What if you made it a bonus conditional on "realized" savings?
Ms. Gomez: Let me think about that for next year.
Vanessa: Well, I'm out of options, so I need your advice. I enjoy working here, and my preference would be to continue. But I'm having increasing trouble paying for my child's college tuition on my current salary. My representative in Human Resources has alerted me to a job opening in the sales department that would provide the extra funds I need. But I'd prefer to stay here and work with you. Is there any way we could work this out this year?

With that, Vanessa's boss realized that losing Vanessa would be far more costly than consenting to a bonus based on the realized savings her efforts would create. Ms. Gomez crossed Vanessa's golden bridge; Vanessa earned a bonus more than adequate to cover the costs of her child's college tuition.

Dealing with the Accidentally Difficult Person

Accidentally difficult people try to do their best but are pulled in two directions. Often, it's a middle manager who wants to meet goals set from higher up, while also being fair to subordinates. If you've ever felt "caught between a rock and a hard place," you may have been an accidentally difficult person. Such people can't see win-win solutions, so you have to help them along—frequently, they are grateful.

POWER MOVES WHEN NEGOTIATING WITH ACCIDENTALLY DIFFICULT PEOPLE

1. **Diagnose—don't react.** Accidentally difficult people often shock us by how quickly they dead-end our requests and ignore our needs. Under pressures of their own, they show no sympathy for ours. Because their negative responses come so quickly and so completely, we are apt to think, "This person is impossible to work with!" "My boss doesn't care about my needs at all." If you find yourself suddenly exasperated, go to the balcony, let tensions subside, strategize about how to get what you need by fulfilling their needs.

    Michelle, a retail buyer, is requesting a week off to deal with her mom's unexpected illness; unfortunately, it's right in the middle of her firm's busiest season.

    "I'm really sorry," says her supervisor, "but at this time of year, the answer is no." The supervisor's win-lose approach only views Michelle's request as incompatible with company needs.

2. **Disarm—consider their perspective and show them you're on their side.** This type of negotiator doesn't think innovatively or expect that others will. They don't see themselves as difficult; they're trying to do the "right" thing. Challengers are seen as unreasonable, uninformed, or, worse, incompetent. But if you acknowledge and work with their pressures, you can bring them to your side.

    After thinking through her boss's seasonal pressures, Michelle emails: "I've come up with a solution. I can attend to my mom's needs and make sure all your workload needs are addressed. May we meet at 3 p.m.?"

3. **Reframe—change the game.** Brainstorm how to satisfy each other's needs. You don't even need to ask permission to do this. Most accidentally difficult people are open to any help they can get, and will change direction if something seems to work better.

   Michelle arrives at her supervisor's office promptly at 3 p.m.

   "Help me understand the pressures you are under," Michelle says. "What needs to be done in the next two weeks?"

   Her supervisor outlines a series of tasks, admittedly a heavy load. "I would never leave you in the lurch at a time like this; I hope you know that," she says. "I am confident I can get these things done and still squeeze in some time with my mom. Will you work with me on this?"

   The supervisor, touched by Michelle's obvious responsiveness to corporate needs, acquiesces to a collaborative approach.

4. **Build a golden bridge—make it easy to say yes.** Accidentally difficult people respond well when you recognize their unmet needs. Empathizing with the reasons behind their "unreasonable" demands is key. Be particularly sensitive to helping them save face, if necessary, especially if you're setting a new precedent.

   Michelle lays out her plan. "If I work overtime before and after the days off, and if I am gone for three days instead of five, I can get all the work done. I can leave on a Thursday and return on a Tuesday; then two of those days are weekend days. And my working overtime will show my coworkers that I'm not getting preferential treatment; I still have to do the work. What else would you need me to do?"

   Her supervisor says Michelle will need to check in while she's gone: "And on the weekends, too, because that may be needed." She is also to work a minimum of two overtime hours each day leading up to the days off plus whatever extra hours might still be needed when she returns. Her supervisor now knows the work will get done, and no dangerous precedents have been set. Michelle's days off are granted.

Dealing with the Unfulfilled Difficult Person

The unfulfilled difficult person will make you feel like your offer is inadequate. Beware of extending your offer with the wrong things. The money and tangible perks may be more than adequate; don't increase these until you've ascertained the person's intangible needs.

POWER MOVES WHEN NEGOTIATING WITH UNFULFILLED DIFFICULT PEOPLE

1. **Diagnose—don't react.** Resistance is the hallmark of the unfulfilled difficult person. This negotiator has unmet needs that she may or may not reveal; dealing with these is perhaps your greatest challenge. The resistance may be very apparent ("Absolutely not! No way!"), or tepid ("Maybe . . . ."), or downright subtle ("I'll have to see about that . . . ."). Diagnosing what's behind it takes time.

    Ernestine is thrilled to have the opportunity to purchase her chief competitor Melanie's consulting business. Although they have competed on numerous bids, they are friendly colleagues with a deep respect for each other's talents.

    Melanie's husband has just retired and wants to travel with her. When Melanie mentions this, Ernestine offers to buy the firm. "We're prepared to make you an offer in the neighborhood of $10 million," Ernestine says.

    Melanie exhales sharply. Surprised, Ernestine thinks Melanie is dissatisfied even though the offer is a generous one. "Are you offering anything else?" asks Melanie. "I'm . . . just not sure at all."

    Ernestine replies that she hasn't included any extras and asks whether there are some things that might sweeten the deal for Melanie. "I don't know," she replies, "I'll have to think about it carefully." They shake hands and agree to meet in two weeks.

    Melanie reschedules this appointment twice.

2. **Disarm them—consider their perspective and show them you're on their side.** With the unfulfilled difficult person, empathy is often

more like mind-reading. Try to get as much information as you can. Try putting yourself in her position; what would you want under similar circumstances?

When Melanie calls to reschedule for the second time, Ernestine realizes something is up. "Are you having second thoughts, Melanie?" she asks.

"No! No!" says Melanie. "I just . . . your offer is generous, but I don't know . . . I feel like something else needs to be in the mix."

"What else might you find enticing?" asks Ernestine.

"Nothing comes right to mind," replies Melanie.

"What are your concerns for the firm after you've sold it?" asks Ernestine, trying to dig deeper.

"I really want it to be run with the same passion, the same concern for my people. Some of them have been with me for their entire careers. I've started projects that need to be continued, and I want my clients to be taken proper care of during and after the transition. I can't address these things if I'm gone, and I care about these things as much as I care about the monetary offer," says Melanie.

Ernestine acknowledges Melanie. "What I hear is that you want your firm, your creation, to be run as you have been running it, that it remain successful. Is that right?"

"Yes!" replies Melanie quickly.

"I feel exactly the same way about my business, Melanie. I've invested thousands of hours in the well-being of my clients, and I could never just take the money and run," says Ernestine, adopting Melanie's perspective with grace and empathy.

3. **Reframe—change the game.** If the unfulfilled difficult person has sound business reasons for not cooperating, those have to be understood and respected before there can be any forward movement. It's also possible that the person's hidden agenda may be entirely personal; more likely, it's a mix of personal and professional. Address these concerns *before* addressing the tangibles. What are their fears? What do they stand to lose? What risks are they facing? Do they know you well enough to have confidence

in your performance? Are they afraid of looking bad in front of people whose opinions they value? Probe to uncover these concerns.

Ernestine now has insight into what's driving Melanie. "You know how we run our business; we share your values about how to treat clients. If that is a concern, we can easily alleviate it." Melanie hastens to assure Ernestine that that is not an issue.

Hmm, then that's not the core issue, Ernestine thinks to herself, and tries again. "Then what do you fear you'll lose if you make a deal?" she asks Melanie.

Melanie pauses a long time. "Losing control of the quality of the work, not having the power to keep things on track, even though my name will be associated with the business for a long while after it's sold, and just . . . not being able to say I'm a business owner anymore, I guess," she says.

Now Ernestine realizes that she has to de-emphasize her monetary offer and collaborate to address Melanie's fears—loss of control, loss of power, loss of status. But how?

4. **Build a golden bridge—make it easy to say yes.** Intangible needs have everything to do with ego and self-esteem. It may cost you little or nothing to address such needs, if you think outside the box about options and alternative approaches.

It is now clear that Melanie is reluctant to sell because she is reluctant to face the loss of control, power, and status. Ernestine sees an easy solution, and one that also provides many pluses to the combined firm.

"Melanie, would you consider staying on board as chairperson emeritus? We could certainly use your steady hand at the helm, but it would allow you to travel with your husband as frequently as you wanted."

Melanie responds with her first show of enthusiasm. "That makes perfect sense! I'd really love that. I could do what I'm good at, while jettisoning all the daily operations. Does your $10 million offer still stand? And what would my chairperson emeritus compensation package look like?"

Melanie and Ernestine complete the acquisition eight weeks later, enthusiastic about their future together.

As I've mentioned, 80 percent of negotiation success lies in the planning stage. You can prepare yourself before engaging with a difficult person by using the following worksheet.

A Planning Worksheet for Negotiating with Difficult People

Express Appreciation

Where can you learn about things they have done that deserve merit and that you can acknowledge and appreciate them for?

1. What questions can you ask to better understand and find merit in what they think, feel, and have done?
2. How might you communicate your newfound knowledge?

Establish Connection

3. What common interests might you discuss?
4. How will you establish yourselves as joint problem-solvers?
5. What might you say or ask to connect on a personal level?

Respect Their Individuality

6. What process might you suggest to structure the negotiation?
7. What habits of yours detract? (For instance, do you talk too much? Listen too little?)
8. How can you check this behavior?

Acknowledge Their Rank

9. In what ways do they hold high social status?
10. In what areas of expertise or experience do they hold particularly high status?

Discover Your Personal Values:
Sticking to Your Principles in Challenging Situations

Let's return to the role our values play in guiding us through high-pressure situations like negotiating with difficult people. As noted, we humans tend to capitulate when we are under the gun. Our values will help us hold firm and see things through to a successful conclusion.

Most of us believe we have good values. When things are going well, it's easy to adhere to your principles. How well do they hold up when things are not going your way? Or when there is a risk of losing everything you've worked so hard to achieve? Most revealing, do you stick to your values when no one is looking? When you think you won't get caught?

Consider the following and record your thoughts.

1. Can I look at myself in the mirror and say that I have stayed true to my values under challenging circumstances? Would I admit to myself that I have not?
2. Looking back over your life, describe a situation in which you deviated from your values in order to achieve your goals.
3. How would you handle that situation if you were to face it again?
4. Ask yourself, if minor deviations lead to major ones later on, am I on a slippery slope in that direction now? Am I allowing my lack of ability to deal with difficult people to push me down this slope? What have I learned from this chapter that might help me reverse this trend?

9

Communication Strategies That Create a Level Playing Field

Boys and girls learn different rules about how to behave. Boys, through sports and play scenarios, learn to be competitive and aggressive, a "winning is all that matters" orientation, to think strategically and take risks, how to blame failure on uncontrollable external forces, and how to mask and control emotion.

By contrast, girls, through interpersonal play and scenarios that deemphasize winning and losing, are highly rewarded for "getting along and being nice." Protecting friendships, helping others, creating win-win situations, being kind and thoughtful, being self-sacrificing, and taking personal responsibility for failure—all these are the lubricants of civilized society. They are ineffective, however, in the face of competitiveness and aggression.

Table 9.1 succinctly outlines our traditional communication differences by gender.

It is important to note here that there also are women—I call them bully women—who have made a study of the competitive, win-lose negotiation style and deploy it regularly. Depending on their upbringing, they tend to be slightly more open to creating win-win situations than men are. However, when negotiating with such women, use the same methods outlined in this chapter as you would when dealing with men.

TABLE 9.1 TRADITIONAL COMMUNICATION DIFFERENCES BY GENDER

MALE	FEMALE
Leadership by command and control: maintain the hierarchy	Leadership through involvement: maintain flatness
Wide range of aggressiveness acceptable	Narrow band of aggressiveness acceptable
Definition of team player: know your slot and play it	Definition of team player: help others, keep things flat
Friendliness: comes and goes	Friendship: lasts beyond time and place
Attacking: hey, it's part of the game, no grudges held	Attacking: taken personally, hurt feelings
Meeting happens *before* the meeting	Meeting happens *in* the meeting
Meetings: speak at length, interrupt	Meetings: share time, wait for turn
Make it up, figure it out later	Go for confessional; share shortcomings
Attribute success to intrinsic factors	Attribute success to outside forces: luck, effort, assistance, support
Failures are for reasons beyond control	Take personal ownership of failures
Avoid disclaimers; maintain sense of certainty in verbal communications	Use disclaimers and tag questions to maintain flatness when communicating
Engage in verbal bantering/teasing to bond	May view banter as cruel, insensitive
Nonverbals: mask emotions, stand shoulder-to-shoulder when speaking, nod to indicate agreement	Nonverbals: show feelings, do "face work," nod to indicate listening
Not a matter of right or wrong. Only different rules and reasons for doing!	

Both male and female cultural orientations bring important skills to the workplace. For example, on scene at an urgent search-and-rescue mission, the command-and-control leadership style associated with the military (or similar male business hierarchy) works most effectively in time-critical situations. One person needs to be in control; others need to obey and fulfill their specific roles. The male cultural orientation—whether exercised by a man or a woman—is best for making effective and efficient rescues. Back in the operations center, the supervisor needs to gather the expertise and ideas of everyone on that watch; here, leadership is based on involvement and multiple inputs. The female cultural orientation—again whether exercised by a man or a woman—works most effectively here, where creativity, psychological team effort, and win-win thinking are required for success.

Women gravitate to workplaces and careers that need and encourage their skill sets; but the higher up the ladder you climb, the more female cultural values clash with the demands of the boardroom. One big component of the so-called glass ceiling is women's lack of negotiation training. Traditional negotiation techniques were created by men for dealing with other men, and women are usually discouraged from learning and practicing these rules. When we do, we're frequently punished for being "unfeminine."

So let's level the playing field with a few rules of our own. Here are some methods that will put you in control, preserve your feminine values, and make the negotiation environment feel less foreign.

The Role of Gender Attitudes Toward Winning

Men want to win.

So do women (who doesn't!), but a man's (and bully woman's) definition of winning relates to achieving goals at any cost whereas a woman's definition of winning relates to achieving win-win results through fostering the relationship with the negotiation partner. "Let the boy win," or "give the man what he wants," is the prevalent attitude toward men; alternatively, self-sacrifice is rewarded in women. But this is outmoded behavior; going forward, we need to create win-win situations together. This requires understanding men's goals and figuring out a way to help men achieve them *while achieving your own goals too*. It means receiving something back for every concession you make, rather than sacrificing your goals for theirs.

How to Gain Control of a Negotiation

Myth: You enter a negotiation with the strategy of responding to what the other party says or does.

Reality: That strategy is far too passive; you've already sacrificed too much power. Instead, as soon as you sit down, set the tone. Say something like, "Let's identify each other's interests, and make a joint effort to create a win-win here." This provides the lead, *your* lead, for how things are going to go; frequently, the other party will follow. If the other party jumps in ahead of you, agree with everything you reasonably can and then add additional lead goals.

Start by making a series of easy-to-agree-with statements. "We're here to produce the best possible outcome." "Our goal is an amicable and fair agreement." "We've already identified a lot of common ground between us." "Our intention is to reach a mutually acceptable agreement as soon as possible." Get your opponent in the habit of agreeing.

If you can manage to take responsibility for setting and disseminating the agenda, grab it. It gives you an important degree of control. What you include (and leave out) can have tremendous impact on a negotiation's success or failure. Even if you can't do this directly, contact the assigned agenda-setter in advance of your meeting to encourage inclusion and exclusion of issues important to you. Remember that all agendas are negotiable; if someone takes complete control of the agenda and ignores your requests, make agenda negotiation your first order of business. You are not bound by your counterpart's rules; demonstrate why it might be in that person's interest to be flexible.

What to Do When Problems Arise

Your counterparts want something that is impossibly difficult. Your natural human response is: "We can't do that; it's not acceptable because X, Y, and Z." You want them to hear and respond to X, Y, and Z. Unfortunately, humans don't readily process information that way. What they'll hear is "We can't do that" and the rest is lost in the emerging frustration.

REASONS COME FIRST

Train yourself (and it will take some training) to state your reasons first and then your problem. Which of the following sounds more competent and likely to keep the lines of communication open?

A: We can't fulfill your order in your two-week time frame. We're entering our busiest season right now, and we just lost one of our maintenance crew so we're training a new one.

B: We're entering our busiest season right now, and we just lost one of our maintenance crew so we're training a new one. Because of all this, we can't fulfill your order in your two-week time frame.

"A" sounds like you're making whiny excuses; "B" sounds like you are presenting a realistic business condition. The language is the same, but "B" states reasons first, and then the problem. This is a very powerful communications tool for leveling the playing field when negotiating with men or bully women who push for concessions whether they need them or not. Just state the facts, ma'am, followed by what you will, won't, or can't agree to.

BANISH THE "BUTS"

Related to the previous situation is the "Yes, but . . ." language habit. It, too, is saying no with whiny excuses. It must go! Just stop at yes. For example, which answer to the question, "Can you fulfill our order in two weeks?" sounds more competent?

A: Yes, but we can't put on additional people to meet your deadline without raising prices.

B: Yes. Adding additional people to meet your deadline is certainly possible. Let's discuss the impact on price and whether deadline or budget is your more important consideration.

Say yes when you can. "Yes" keeps negotiations flowing and leads to innovative solutions. "But" stalls negotiations and creates frustration. Your counterparts do not feel their concerns have been heard if you say, "Yes, but." "Yes" is the most powerful way to disarm a win-lose-oriented counterpart. "Yes" is the win a man (and bully woman) seeks; you're giving them what they want.

Test Assumptions, Broad Statements, and Mutual Understanding

If you assume your counterpart defines something the way you do, you are sowing the seeds of a failed agreement. Remember, men and women belong to different cultures, and cultures can define even the most common things very differently. For instance, men do not assume relationships are top priority in negotiations. Women frequently do. If you assume a male negotiator ought to hold relationships in high priority, and he does not, your assumption will cause you to get angry, and you will lose your ability to strategize on your feet. This is just one type of assumption that needs to be tested.

All broad statements and mutual "understandings" should be tested and clarified throughout negotiations. Here's an example of how to break up an impasse using the testing and clarification method:

Your opponent: Your people are always late with your orders.

You: Are you saying we are all late all of the time?

Your opponent: Well, no, not everyone, it's usually the electrical department.

You: Do you mean all the people in the electrical department?

Your opponent: I suppose not; we tend to deal with Joe, and he is often late, but Fred and Harry are generally okay.

You: And does Joe tend to be late all of the time, or is it at particular times?

Your opponent: The problem is generally during overhauls. I know Joe is the busiest, but it's causing us some problems.

You: Let me make sure I understand the problem: It is the speed of Joe's response in the electrical department during overhauls that is giving you the most cause for concern.

Your opponent: Yes.

You: Well, that's very helpful and allows me to do something about it straightaway. If I came back to you with a proposal by this time next week, would that help to solve your problems?

Your opponent: Yes, definitely.

Here, a win-win situation has been created out of an impasse because the problem as stated was tested until it became sharply defined. Frustration breeds generalization; cooler heads manage perceptions and define and solve problems. Competitive negotiators who use anger as a tool can be brought under control by testing assumptions, generalizations, and understanding.

One way to test assumptions is to summarize. "Before we move on to other things, let's just make sure we are clear on the things we've already agreed to . . . ." Competitive negotiators may take this as an opportunity to renegotiate or demand more concessions; be firm about holding to agreements, but also recognize that summarizing can reveal differing assumptions, which can then be addressed before they cause problems.

How to Make Acceptable Counterproposals

Immediate counterproposals sound like saying no. Your "no" will be heard and elicit a frustration response; the facts of the counterproposal will not be heard well, or at all.

Everyone likes to receive validation. So before you launch into the points of a counterproposal, first acknowledge the validity of the other side's arguments. "I think your arguments are quite compelling. Let me see if I understand completely what you are proposing . . . ."

Once your opponents know you've heard and agreed with their point, they will be much more open to ways in which you prefer to expand the deal. Once again, competitive negotiators always go for the "yes"; validation is a powerful "yes." You've placed them in the winner's circle, and positioned them adroitly for a nudge into collaboration. Even if your counterproposals conflict with what they want, you can seize the opportunity to make them seem like added benefits. This is easier to do when the audience is receptive!

Avoid Diluting Your Arguments

"I had a thousand reasons for having the risk team take on this project," cried Sandra. "But they wouldn't listen and denied my request!"

Sandra's "thousand" reasons actually diluted her case. People can hear only so many reasons before they shut down and don't remember any. Stick with your top two or three. Pound them home; repeat as necessary.

Also, if you stick with your strongest reasons, you are less likely to become the victim of a competitive negotiator who finds ways to pick apart your weaker reasons. That makes all your arguments seem weak and dismissible. Stick with your top two or three. Pound them home; repeat as necessary.

How to Defend Against Gender Bias

A new study conducted by researchers Laura J. Kray and Alex B. Van Zant of the University of California, Berkeley, and Jessica A. Kennedy of the University of Pennsylvania found that people are more likely to lie to female negotiators than to male negotiators because they see women as less competent than men, thus less likely to question their lies. The study also showed that men negotiators are likely to get preferential treatment by both men and women.[1]

Such biased actions can significantly derail women's negotiated outcomes, putting them at a disadvantage. The question then is, what can women do about it?

The following three nuggets of information will help you achieve better negotiation outcomes:

1. **Take defensive measures.** Women need to know the tactics being used on them and respond appropriately. Create your own level playing field by knowing that for every tactic there is a countertactic or defense.

2. **Be communal.** Approach negotiations from the view of how what you want will benefit the organization and/or team rather than just yourself. This approach conforms to the female stereotype that women are particularly concerned about others.

3. **Be assertive but gracious.** It is important to combine an assertive message with friendly gestures, smiles, and other nonthreatening and traditionally feminine behavior.

It would be unfair to stop here and rest the burden solely on the shoulders of women. It behooves corporations to remove the impediments to negotiation success for women that they are not in a position to address themselves.

For these reasons, it is imperative that corporations address inequities in the way they perceive and treat women negotiators. The following steps will help corporations blaze a path to real change.

1. **Redefine the rules**. Instead of assigning projects and promotions to those who ask for them, managers should be directed to review the work of all employees at that level, male and female, and inquire across the board about their interests.

2. **Include gender as part of diversity programs.** Companies that include gender as part of their diversity programs are going to be far ahead of the game in attracting the best talent. Doing this shows employees at all levels that the company takes gender equity seriously.

Manage How You See Yourself and How Others See You

True story: A young man came home from Princeton University and told his dad he thought he understood the reason why women were routinely paid less than men. "It's because they don't ask!" he said, shaking his head.

If it's true we get what we expect in this world, then we women need to raise our expectations. The higher your expectations, the greater the likelihood you will get a better result. This means challenging all the old thoughts about being unworthy, unprepared, disadvantaged, of limited resources, and the like. These thoughts place you at a disadvantage in even collaborative negotiations. If you don't expect much for yourself, how can you craft an agreement that expands the pie for both sides?

Competitive negotiators are masters at perceiving and manipulating weakness, and they zero in like hungry buzzards on counterparts with low expectations. They will make you feel grateful for crumbs left behind from the multilayer cake you just gave them. And no, they won't like you better because you let them have the cake while you ate crumbs; they'll think you're an easy mark. (They'll keep coming back to bleed you dry.) So the single most important strength you can develop in yourself is the ability to say "I am worthy of success" and mean it. It's your strongest defensive line against competitive males and bully women; it will enable you to stand strong under pressure and show them they cannot win by bullying. In one stroke, you manage both your perception of yourself *and* their perception of you.

Take a moment to list your beliefs about yourself, the world, and your place in it. If you've never done this before, it is sure to be an eye-opener. It is especially important to write down the negatives, the shames, and the things that make you depressed because you feel there's nothing you can do about them. They look a lot different on paper than they do in your head, and, somehow, they become more challengeable. "That's old." "My mom was wrong about that!" "I'm already more successful than that, but I still feel unworthy. Why? Do I still need to feel that way?"

DO A POWER INVENTORY

It's rare that you'll go into a negotiation where the other party holds all the cards. But too frequently, I see women deferring as if this were the case when they don't need to. It's not just a matter of wanting to please the other side and maintain good relations, it also has to do with not having done their power inventory homework.

When you do your first power inventory, you will be shocked by how much power you actually possess. It also will alert you to areas where you need to do some homework.

The following checklist will help you quickly assess the power you bring to the table:

Power of Information

☐ I have facts and data in my head (or close at hand) that support my desired outcome.

☐ I know how to actively listen, and will collect as much intelligence as I can from my opponent.

☐ I am the only one who can present certain key information.

☐ I am an expert in my field or I am bringing an expert with me.

Power Position

☐ My position is sufficiently high in the organization that it garners respect.

☐ I have achieved status in my industry due to long experience.

☐ I have achieved status in my industry due to awards for my achievements.

☐ I have been appointed or promoted into a position that people respect.

☐ I have formal authority within my organization to rule over certain activities.

☐ I can expect to benefit from reciprocity for value already given.

☐ I have responsibility for the outcome of this deal; it can't get done without my approval.

And if you are fortunate enough:

☐ I was born into a well-respected family that will impress my opponents.

☐ I hold an elected office that wields power over the outcome of this negotiation.

❐ I hold some type of equity or ownership that ensures me a vote or a say.

Power of Resources
❐ I control and dispense money.
❐ I control and dispense supplies.
❐ I control and dispense human resources.
❐ I control and dispense time.
❐ I control and dispense equipment.
❐ I control and dispense critical services.
❐ I control and dispense interpersonal support.
❐ I manage a stockpile of needed resources.
❐ I have other resources to which I can go if I need to walk away from this deal.

Power of Relationships
❐ I can define the goals of this negotiation.
❐ I have much in common with my counterparts, increasing my persuasive ability over them.
❐ My network of relationships impacts who gets to know what information.
❐ My network of relationships impacts who receives goods and services promptly.
❐ My network of relationships could provide valuable contacts to my counterpart.
❐ I have strong and/or lengthy relationships with important parties to this negotiation.
❐ I am a good coalition builder.

You have convinced yourself you deserve success. You've accurately assessed the full extent of your power. Get out there and use it, graciously and without embarrassment, on your newly leveled playing field!

Discover Your Negotiation Skills:
Know the Difference

To keep the playing field on an even keel, the first step is to make sure you adjust your communication style to the one that best suits the hearer. As we've seen, there are differences in the ways in which most men and women communicate, and though we may wish that weren't so, to succeed in the real world, it's important that we recognize the differences and use them to achieve the results we want.

The following brief exercise will tell you how well you can identify the style differences between men and women. Circle your answer. Then compare your answers to those in the answer key that follows.

COMMUNICATION STYLES		
1. Decide quickly based on the content they hear	Women	Men
2. Take in the speaker's words to determine the message's meaning	Women	Men
3. Interrupt less often	Women	Men
4. Prefer that the speaker get to the point quickly	Women	Men
5. Hear the words and the emotions or feelings behind the words	Women	Men
6. Stand face-to-face, looking at the person's face	Women	Men
7. Acknowledge the speaker by making short comments such as "I agree"	Women	Men
8. Gather information from body language and other clues as well as words before making a decision	Women	Men
9. Hear the words and the content	Women	Men
10. Take longer to decide	Women	Men

ANSWER KEY	
1. Men	6. Women
2. Men	7. Women
3. Women	8. Women
4. Men	9. Men
5. Women	10. Women

10

Fail-Proof Persuasion Tactics

As you'll realize when reading this chapter, you are already a persuasive person. You've instinctively used many of these tactics to obtain what you want since childhood. By recognizing, defining, and practicing them, you create tools you can use on the job. More important, you'll know when such techniques are being directed at you and can then respond to or deflect them. You'll never again be at the mercy of persuasive manipulators.

Persuasion is a five-step process:

Step 1. Establish credibility
Step 2. Create common ground
Step 3. Provide vivid evidence that your request will create value
Step 4. Connect emotionally
Step 5. Take action

Use the quick checklist on the next page to help strategize your approach.

Persuasion Process

1. ESTABLISH CREDIBILITY

- ☐ Expertise/Knowledge
- ☐ Strong Relationships
- ☐ Listening to Others
- ☐ History of Good Judgment

2. FIND COMMON GROUND

- ☐ Clarify the Benefits
- ☐ Offer Mutually Beneficial Solutions
- ☐ Illuminate the Advantages
- ☐ Understand Other Views

3. PROVIDE VIVID EVIDENCE

- ☐ Imagery and Metaphors
- ☐ Stories and Examples
- ☐ Spreadsheets/Statistics

4. CONNECT EMOTIONALLY

- ☐ Understand the Emotions
- ☐ Show Empathy
- ☐ Demonstrate Commitment
- ☐ Be Self-Aware

5. TAKE ACTION

- ☐ Suggest Next Steps

Six Persuasive Tactics to Optimize Your
Negotiating Prowess

To gain an edge in a negotiation, apply these six primary persuasive tactics as needed:

1. **Hero Strategy:** Ask the person with whom you are negotiating for advice (men love to feel like heroes; women love to feel helpful). Win counterparts over by making them feel important.
2. **Rational Persuasion Tactic:** Use logic and factual data to persuade others that a specific course of action will lead to desirable outcomes.
3. **Inspirational Appeal Technique:** Create motivation by focusing on their ideals, aspirations, and values.
4. **Morality Appeal Strategy:** Motivate their desire to do the right thing.
5. **Coalition Tactic:** Enlist the help of others who might, alone or as a group, have more power to persuade than you do.
6. **Reciprocity Technique:** "You scratch my back, and I'll scratch yours."

HERO STRATEGY

Every woman has felt it. Every woman hates it. That weird, uncomfortable feeling you get when you know a man is interested in more than just doing business with you. That is the situation I found myself in with Dave—a high-profile executive with decision-making power, who could help me take my business to the next level. Dave had asked me to drinks to discuss "potential business," but I sensed he had another agenda. I would have to reject him, which would hurt his ego and hinder our ability to do business.

To salvage the relationship, I knew I had to think fast, be smart, and handle the situation strategically. I was clear on my two objectives: (1) to tactically protect Dave's ego by making sure he "saved face" and (2) to make sure my strategy supported and preserved his interest in doing business with me.

In negotiations, especially with men, saving an opponent's face—his public image, reputation, and status—is a negotiator's most valuable skill. It is important to take the ego issue off the table in order to negotiate successfully. Saving face is a way to let someone out of an embarrassing or compromising situation with dignity intact.

By the time I walked into the restaurant I knew exactly what I had to do.

> *Yasmin:* Hi, Dave, I'm so glad you're here. I really need your advice.
> *Dave:* Of course.
> *Yasmin:* A dear friend of mine finds herself in a difficult and uncomfortable situation with a client who is acting inappropriately. You are a man of great integrity—something I highly admire—so I thought you could advise me about what my friend should do.
> *Dave:* What your friend's client is doing is completely unacceptable.

By now, Dave was on a roll. I had appealed to the hero in him.

> *Dave:* She needs to put him in his place, or he won't stop.
> *Yasmin:* Thanks, Dave. I'll tell my friend to do exactly that.

The rest of the evening was pure business and Dave became my client that night.

Whether or not I was correct about Dave's original intentions no longer mattered. By strategically influencing *how Dave saw himself*, I had given him a more important role—the role of "hero," which he felt compelled to live up to.

RATIONAL PERSUASION TACTIC

This tactic enlists the power of logic and facts. If you do A, B, and C, you will benefit in X, Y, and Z ways. It is effective with many, but not all, people. For those whose decision-making process is ruled more by intuition or emotion than known facts, it can create resistance and stalling.

If your negotiating partner is receptive to facts and logical thinking, you might rationally persuade him or her by explaining:

- **Why an action needs to occur.** The needs it will meet, why doing it is important.
- **What the benefits are.** Answer the unspoken question, "What's in it for me?"
- **Why it will succeed.** Motivate accomplishment by providing details, step-by-step plans, and case studies.
- **How problems and concerns will be handled.** People fear failing in front of colleagues and supervisors. Statements like "That won't happen" or "We don't have to worry about that" only increase anxieties. Anticipate concerns, formulate thorough answers, validate concerns you haven't anticipated, and quickly provide answers.
- **Why your proposal is better than competing plans.** Do your homework and compile a strong list of advantages.

INSPIRATIONAL APPEAL TECHNIQUE

We've all been touched by a passionate speaker, someone whose intense inner convictions ignite the enthusiasms of everyone around her. Such people appeal to your values, ideals, and aspirations, making you believe you can achieve anything. They are less effective, though, at inspiring people who primarily function in a logical way.

All good negotiators inspire both their team and their opponents. The five basic components of an effective inspirational appeal are the ability to:

- **Know the other person's motivating ideals and values.** Human beings all want to feel important, useful, skillful, worthwhile, and able to be the best at something. Negotiators who persuade their opponents that their highest aspirations and your business goals are linked will create win-wins and deeply loyal relationships.

- **Uplift a person's self-concept.** Negotiators can shape how opponents view themselves. Helping others understand their importance while achieving your goals inspires them to go the extra mile.
- **Offer an appealing vision of the future.** Incentives, advancement, personal and professional growth . . . dangle all potential rewards for achieving agreement.
- **Believe in your team *and* your counterpart.** Communicate, positively and optimistically, that you have total faith in everyone's ability to come to an agreement. Especially when dealing with inexperienced team members, self-confidence must be stoked throughout complex negotiations. Remind your counterparts what they have to gain by coming to an agreement.
- **Match your body language to your message.** If you don't, it makes you seem insincere, which makes others anxious and distrustful. If making presentations makes you nervous, use deep stretches, deep breathing, and positive visualization to help your body language reinforce your words. Remember, all the other techniques will fail if you are insincere.

MORALITY APPEAL STRATEGY

Morality and integrity go hand in hand; if you lack integrity, you will never be able to pull off a morality appeal. (You may recall what happened to televangelists who went astray: they quickly disappeared.) Morality appeals are successful only if you are of high moral fiber—someone who can inspire others about the right thing to do, someone others respect or wish to emulate.

You can demonstrate your moral principles by:

- Faithfully adhering to them, even when no one is looking
- Sticking to your guns even when it requires personal sacrifice
- Inspiring your family and friends to validate your moral integrity of their own accord
- "Showing" rather than "crowing"; that is, proving by your actions rather than bragging

In the values exercise at the end of the chapter, you can test the state of your own integrity.

COALITION TACTIC

Very few people in this world possess the power to get what they want, when they want it, all the time. Those who come closest usually have developed strong networks and groups of people who will support them.

So why go it alone? The more people on your side, the more influential you are. From peer-to-peer interactions all the way up to influencing the board of directors, some strategizing and reaching out is all it takes to form a coalition.

Here are some effective ways to use your coalitions:

- **Show a list of supporters** to the person or group you're trying to persuade. List the most influential and least resistant supporters first. Then include those who only partially support you. When those who oppose you see who is on your side, their resistance can soften.
- **Bring supporters to the meeting.** This is critical if you expect resistance. In-person support is the most credible and least refutable way to show who's in favor of your argument.
- **Ask supporters to speak on your behalf.** While a group standing by your side is impressive, their verbal support is even stronger.
- **Enlist behind-the-scenes support.** You may not be able to persuade opponents at the negotiating table, particularly if they are under pressure to win or save face in front of others. But they may be more amenable if someone they respect comes to their office for a private chat . . . or two . . . or three. Persistence overcomes resistance.
- **Call upon the power of a higher authority.** This is the fast track to greater credibility and decreased resistance.

RECIPROCITY TECHNIQUE

Bridge building, good karma, tit-for-tat, whatever you want to call it, doing favors for others in the workplace makes good sense. They can tip the balance when you need someone to go to bat for you, vouch for your integrity, help you find a job, recommend you for a promotion, or join your negotiating team.

Favors aren't always returned: The boss you've been buttering up may leave to join another company and not invite you to join him. But favors have a knack of coming back to you, sometimes in unexpected ways; for example: Your day off that a colleague promised to cover may be ruined by a big project that can't be put off, but sometime later the colleague surfaces with important statistical or legal data that turns the tide of a negotiation in your favor; or she asks her boss to support your negotiation.

Here are some surefire ways to build reciprocity:

- Take the blame for someone else's error
- Make someone look good by allowing him to take your idea or solution and propose it as his own
- Find someone a new job
- Hire someone's relative
- Be a mentor
- Take on extra tasks to help meet a deadline
- Recommend prospects to the sales department
- Do whatever you can to help others make money

The Seventh Tactic—Reframing

Reframing is the process of shifting the nature of a problem by changing how you look at it. You can redefine the problem, rework how you approach it, or broaden the context in which you describe it. Reframing helps you "think outside the box," and it can be used as part of each of the six other tactics. It's an especially important tool to employ when you've hit a wall and everyone is feeling frustrated.

Here is an example of how reframing works: Charlene, executive vice president of fleet sales for a major automotive company, called her sales team together for an emergency session. She announced: "We're about to lose one of our biggest clients, and we need to prevent this." Her team members employed reframing in several ways; they attempted to:

- **Redefine the words.** Sales associate A responded by redefining the words. "Are we really losing them, or are they just putting out feelers?"
- **Clarify.** Sales associate B addressed the time frame. "How soon are they going to jump ship? Tomorrow? Next week? Next month? When their budget year ends?"
- **Explore the consequences.** Sales associate C asked, "Are they profitable clients, or would we be better off without them and putting more effort into finding a more lucrative client?"
- **Explore other options.** Sales associate D added, "I have two prospects almost ready to sign who are substantially larger than this client. Let's not divert too many resources away from attracting this new business."
- **Go on the offense.** Sales associate E offered, "Perhaps we should threaten to pull out first and leave them in the lurch; it might make them see the value we bring to the table."
- **Examine the evidence.** Sales associate F asked, "How do we know we're about to lose them? Why do you feel this is imminent?"
- **Appeal to the positive.** Sales associate G, who believed that they were about to lose the client, suggested, "It's clear we really care about this client; let's communicate that to them. It's added value and a reminder that our relationship with them has always been solid and proactively responsive."
- **Change the context.** Sales associate H proposed, "If we could get senior management to convince the client that we're in active negotiations to acquire the competitor they're considering going with, they may decide it's safer to stay with the winning team."

Charlene and her team persuaded the client to stay on board. They realized they had about six months to act before the client's budget year ended; by doing their homework, they found out that the client had put out feelers but serious negotiations had not begun. Rather than pulling her entire team into a full-court press effort to retain the client, Charlene assigned the client's two favorite reps to reiterate the value they placed on serving the client. The rest of the team remained focused on bringing in the two bigger clients, one of which signed on in three months. Senior management agreed to approach the competitor with informal merger talks, out of which came more serious long-term strategic plans. No threats to leave the client in the lurch were necessary; a three-year contract was negotiated that was favorable to both sides.

Build Rapport

Persuasion is easier once you've built rapport. Use the other person's name a few times (not too frequently), and be sure you're using it correctly. Use first names only with the person's permission. The equally strong handshake, direct but nonchallenging eye contact, smile, and ability to mirror the other person's speech patterns and body language all go a long way. (Women may find that eye contact, listening, and compliments may convey unintended romantic interest; if you see this happening, excuse yourself, invite someone else into the group, or steer the conversation into neutral territory. On the other hand, these are good female-to-female rapport builders.)

Put away the mobile devices and give the person you are speaking with your undivided attention. Listen to and validate what he or she is saying, seeking common ground. Respond with honesty to establish trust. Then state obvious facts or universal beliefs such as, "It's true that getting a raise is a morale booster" to get the person into the habit of agreeing. You can also employ presuppositions like "As the economy picks up, we'll see profits improve."

You can also use tag questions to get people involved with your ideas, phrasing them so they respond "yes." For example, "As we take more action, our market share goes up, doesn't it?"

Keep the Focus on Your Goals

Sometimes you'll want to hammer home a significant point. Other times, you'll want to divert attention away from something.

To get someone to focus on an important point, repeat and form positive associations. The human brain starts to accept as true something it hears more than once. TV commercials are notorious for using this strategy (New! Improved!). They also exploit positive or negative associations. A handsome man appears at a housewife's door with a product that saves the day. People turn away from someone who's not using the right deodorant.

Conversely, you may want to divert someone's attention from certain aspects of your negotiation. Refrain from mentioning things that weaken your argument (but do so ethically—don't hide vital information, for example, that you don't have the manufacturing capability to fulfill the client's needs).

Confusion can be used to good effect; lawyers are masters of this technique. They'll provide long and elaborately detailed explanations, then feign frustration and aggravation if you ask to walk through the information step by step. Whenever you feel confused during a negotiation, don't just assume it's your fault! Most likely you're being manipulated. Take charge—insist on clear executive summaries (or sow a little lawyer-like, too-much-information confusion back!).

Counter-Persuasion Techniques

Some of the best counter-persuasion techniques that you should learn to recognize, because, of course, they can be used by anyone, come from doctors, who sometimes resort to one or more of the following tactics in order to influence pharmaceutical reps and resist persuasion.

- **Refuse to meet with you.** Or strictly control your access. As a result, a large chunk of your time and effort is devoted to overcoming these obstacles.

- **Remain silent.** Silence is probably the most difficult form of resistance to overcome because it provides no feedback about the effectiveness of your persuasive attempts. Silence might also signal a passive-aggressive personality. Some physicians sit through an entire presentation without saying a word, not even answering questions. Often their body language is difficult to decipher.

- **Seem to acquiesce.** They agree, or pretend to agree, with the rep's statements to shorten the exchange and to instill a false sense of confidence in the rep.

- **Go off on a tangent.** Some physicians will purposely digress in order to disrupt the rep's presentation and the flow of the rep's arguments. They will talk about sports, the weather, the markets, or their travel plans, which takes up the rep's time and prevents him or her from pitching the product persuasively.

- **Create disruptions.** Physicians might deliberately disrupt the flow of the rep's sales pitch. Disruptions can take several forms: answering the phone, talking to a nurse, snacking, or leaving the room for any number of reasons. Even coughing, scratching, or attending to various other body parts can distract the sales rep.

- **Cause interruptions.** Physicians use interruptions as a counter-persuasion ploy, and a way to assert their authority or superiority. Among their tactics are the:
  - *Power interrupt*, start speaking whenever they choose to, even interrupting reps in mid-sentence.
  - *Touch interrupt*, physically touching the rep on his arm or shoulder.
  - *Identity interrupt*, mentioning the rep's name, e.g., "Joe. Listen. Let me make this clear . . . ."
  - *Disinterest interrupt*, indicating a lack of interest in what the rep wants to discuss or claiming that his assertions are impractical, e.g., "Look. This might be important to you, but it's of no value to the patients I see," or "No. I am not willing to talk about how I treat hypertension. What I want to know is . . . ," or "Before you go on any further, the concept might be nice, but it won't work in the real world."

- *Disagreement interrupt*, forcefully disputing what the rep is saying, e.g., "No, no, no! That is completely wrong. The right approach is . . . ."
- **Ask for more data.** Many physicians claim, truthfully or not, that they do not have enough information to start prescribing a new product. They will ask for more clinical trial results, articles, reviews, and other literature. Some will question the research methodology and ask for minute statistical details. Asking lots of relevant and less relevant questions (e.g., splitting hairs) can distract the rep, use up his time, and deflect his persuasive attempts. Some physicians will grill the rep with legitimate or trick questions.
- **Fake anger, cast blame, and attack verbally.** Some physicians try to throw reps off-track by appearing annoyed over some minor detail, taking slight about some small things reps said, or berating them for not knowing some "important facts."
- **Complain and escalate.** Dissatisfied physicians might complain about a rep's behavior to his manager, call his company's head office, or report his action to various government agencies. Others threaten to do this in order to gain concessions.
- **Grab the moral high ground.** Some accuse a rep of being dishonest or unethical for suggesting something they perceive as illegal or inappropriate. Crying foul and stating that they would never do such an immoral thing can be a convenient way to dismiss reps' requests and thwart their persuasive attempts. Also, taking a moral high ground puts the doctor in a position of superiority and forces the rep to retreat and seek forgiveness.
- **Refer to a higher authority.** Physicians can also dodge making a decision by invoking a higher authority and the need to consult with other decision-makers, such as colleagues, department heads, or formulary managers. The "higher authority" excuse also implies the existence of a tougher negotiator and may be used as a threat to get the rep to offer more concessions.
- **Befriend the rep.** Some succeed in befriending many reps and developing really close ties with some of them. These strong personal

relationships can become quite touchy. For example, some reps will start feeling uncomfortable with the idea of "selling to friends." Others will be tempted to unfairly favor their physician friends and ignore others.

Discover Your Personal Values:
How Well Do You Practice Integrity?

Integrity consists of sincerity, consistency, and substance. If you have not always acted with integrity in the workplace, you are not alone. Integrity is built one action at a time and soon becomes a habit.

There are numerous power, status, and productivity pressures that create rule-bending temptations. You may feel your job is in jeopardy. Your boss may say "the ends justify the means" when conscience-tweaking actions erode one's integrity. But this trend can be reversed with courage and polite (but firm) persistence.

To see where you fall on the integrity scale, answer the following questions; then make improvements as needed:

Sincerity

Do I:

- ❒ Put up a false front?
- ❒ Accept responsibility for my commitments and strive to meet them?
- ❒ Honestly admit my own limitations?
- ❒ Accept responsibility for my mistakes?
- ❒ Tell the truth?

Consistency

Do I:

- ❒ Treat people equally?
- ❒ Follow through on all my promises?
- ❒ Work as hard as or harder than expected?
- ❒ Have the same expectations and rules for myself as I have for others?

Substance

Do I:

- ☐ Keep private information private?
- ☐ Refrain from gossiping and complaining about others?
- ☐ Do what's best for the team, and not just what's best for me?
- ☐ Give credit where credit is due?
- ☐ Care about the development of the people who work for me?
- ☐ Make it a priority to keep the lines of communication open and resolve any conflicts?

11

The Art of the Redirect:
Managing Destabilizing Moves

Recognizing a move for what it is—a tactic that is intended to diminish you and shift power to the other side—allows you to respond deliberately and strategically with a redirect.

This chapter will empower you against diminishing moves—the ones that make you doubt yourself, or that cause others to doubt you, your abilities, or your expertise. The following are the negative moves opponents of both sexes commonly make on women:

- **Challenging your competence or expertise.** Your experience or expertise is questioned. Your opinion, position, or service is devalued, for example: "Your fees are way out of line with what you deliver."
- **Demeaning your ideas.** Your ideas are attacked in ways that give you little room to respond, making the idea (and you) sound ridiculous: "You can't be serious about this proposal."
- **Criticizing your style.** You are cast as a person who cannot be reasoned with, or is selfish, or not nice. You might be categorized as inconsistent, irrational, or hypersensitive. Examples: "Don't get so upset." "You are so greedy." "Stop being so difficult." Even "calm down" can be subtly unsettling.

- **Making threats.** These assertions of power are designed to back you into a corner, or to try to force a choice. Phrases like "Cut your rates or there is no deal" make it risky even to propose another solution.

Counter the Sublevel Negotiation with Redirects

In best-practice negotiation, participants focus on crafting agreements that meet mutual needs, create win-win scenarios, and foster solid business relationships.

That's on the surface.

There is a sublevel to all negotiations where raw power dynamics rule the day; these affect whether and how your ideas are heard, credited, and shaped into an agreement. Consider these two cases:

- The vice president of a company's global ventures is in negotiation with the vice president of European operations to close down a non-performing subsidiary. The VP of European operations agrees to take on the project. When nothing happens for months, the VP of global ventures confronts her negotiating partner on the phone. "Calm down," he tells her. "You're overreacting."
- An independent service provider is negotiating a contract renewal with a valued client. To his surprise, the client claims the rates are way out of line with what the provider delivers and threatens to hire someone else.

In both cases, one party is making a move to control the negotiation by challenging the other party's legitimacy and credibility. The natural response is to become defensive, which weakens your ability to strategically advocate for your own interests and concerns. Instead, you need to operate on the sublevel.

As you negotiate issues like price and performance, you also are negotiating power. This is done by managing others' impression of you, claiming and maintaining all your legitimacy and credibility, asserting genuine influence, and shaping perceptions of issues and problems. "Moves" are challenges to these; "redirects" are responses that neutralize moves. *The better you're able to identify moves and fend them off with redirects, the greater your chances of successful negotiation.*

THE MOST INSIDIOUS MOVES

So far the moves I've described are overtly aggressive. The more subtle—and insidious—moves are those that flatter or appeal to your sympathy. For example, following a year of excellent performance and added responsibility, a marketing director schedules a meeting to negotiate her salary and bonus with her boss. Expecting a favorable outcome, she is thrown off guard when her boss says, "Times are tight; I know I can count on you to drop this for now."

Five Redirects to Counter Any Move

Most women struggle with how to respond to moves. They're tricky. If you ignore them, you've sent the message that your opponents can successfully "play" you. But if you confront them, you risk escalating the situation or playing into their hands. For example, if you respond to "Don't get so upset" by shouting "I'm not upset!" you have confirmed their positioning of you as excessively emotional and irrational. Either way, you're on the defensive.

The only way out is to recognize a move for what it is—an attempt to destabilize you and shift power to them. Doing so allows you to retain your power with the most strategically disarming redirect. Redirects demonstrate you don't accept another's definition of you. "Upset?" you might say quizzically. The onus is then on them to prove their point. Or switch the conversation back onto the issues: "Let's not get stuck on me; we have a problem to deal with." No defensiveness needed!

Redirects can be either restorative (helping you regain power or credibility) or participative (creating space for your opponent to respond legitimately by phrasing your response in a collaborative way).

If you do nothing with this book but memorize the following five redirects, you will make yourself an exponentially better negotiator:

REDIRECT 1: INSERT TIME OR SPACE

To disrupt the almost hypnotic power of a move, interrupt it by inserting time and/or space. Even a few seconds will help shift the balance of power. In the example above, after the VP of European operations tells the VP of global ventures to calm down, her response should be to put the phone on hold for a moment (perhaps by creating an "unavoidable interruption"), giving both parties time to regain emotional control.

How to Do It Firmly and Without Disruption Katherine had just been appointed head of her company's financial review committee. Salli, another member, had actively campaigned for the job and resented Katherine. Katherine had called an initial meeting of all the committee members to discuss how to proceed. Salli rushes in, apologizing for being late, and begins to pass out a four-page financial strategy handout, in an attempt to usurp Katherine's role as chair. Katherine smiles at Salli. "What a lot of work," Katherine says, picking up her coffee mug. "Anyone else want a refill?"

Following Katherine's lead, the committee members get up and congregate around the coffee pot; the "time-out" destroyed the focus on Salli's memo. When the group reassembles, Katherine is ready. "We are not as far along as you, Salli," Katherine says. "We haven't yet identified the approach we want to take, much less set priorities. Perhaps it would be better to review your memo for any pertinent ideas after the committee establishes these."

When Katherine inserted time and space into this challenge from Salli, she accomplished several positive things:

- She prevented herself from being rude to a committee member who had obviously put in a lot of effort.
- She prevented Salli's memo from dominating the committee's discussion, and Salli from taking control of the session.
- She subtly but effectively communicated to Salli who was in charge.

REDIRECT 2: LABEL THE MOVE

Demonstrate that you recognize a move for what it is, and you've instantly gained respect. When an independent service provider is told his client will switch to another provider, he can name the move: "You and I both know that would create more work for you." Threat neutralized, power equalized.

How to Do It Powerfully Some moves are ethically, morally, or legally unacceptable; naming (and shaming) them is a strong and effective power move. Mallica's community arts center had restored pride and vitality to an inner-city neighborhood. Always on a tight budget, Mallica was jubilant when *60 Minutes* floated tentative plans to tape a segment on inner-city revitalization at the center.

The construction union, however, immediately recognized an opportunity. The union knew that segment producers would scuttle the program if unresolved labor disputes produced picket lines. Union personnel made their moves to force Mallica to make the center's construction projects all-union; for them it was business as usual.

Mallica called it blackmail. "I was very angry," she said. "The union needed to understand that we were personally and institutionally very disappointed. I was not going to downplay that. They violated a trust. I told the union leader that we understood their game, disrespected it, and condemned them for their shortsightedness. The head of the Local, who lives in the area, had tears in his eyes after I finished talking to him."

Mallica's redirect caught the union in an opportunistic play that hurt rather than helped its membership; union officials backed down.

REDIRECT 3: QUESTION THE MOVE

A question throws the burden back on the mover. It says the move seems puzzling, or unprovoked, but not especially anger-inducing. In negotiating her salary, the marketing director might use a questioning redirect with her boss: "If you were in my position, I wonder how you would respond to the request you just made?"

How to Do It Without Harming Yourself I have yet to meet the professional woman who has not at some time had to deal with demeaning moves. These call attention to a woman's anatomy and away from her professional abilities. They employ seemingly flattering words like "babe" and "sweetheart," or so-called compliments that allow the perpetrator to act hurt if rebuffed. Deflecting these can make a woman look churlish, humorless, or mean-spirited; yet if she does not respond, the label sticks and the invitation to further challenges remains open. These things have to be stopped dead in their tracks, and success depends to a great extent on your delivery—wit, inflection, raised eyebrow.

Before a major sales presentation, a young actuary hears a stage whisper: "She can run my numbers anytime." That sotto voce commentary is not a compliment. It's a deliberate move to put the actuary "in her place."

Having learned from experience to be prepared for such remarks, the actuary has a retort handy: "Would you repeat that? Yes, you in the red tie. I couldn't hear." Suggestiveness and innuendo, she finds, don't survive repetition, and questioning puts the perpetrators in *their* place. With demeaning moves, it is critical to act quickly and decisively from a place of unruffled strength.

REDIRECT 4: CORRECT THE MOVE

Opponents make moves when they think they can benefit by attributing negative qualities or motivations to you. When a service provider is told, "Your fees are way out of line with the service you provide," he is cast as a price gouger offering an inferior product. Merely rejecting this definition increases tensions; substituting a new and better definition neutralizes them. By being prepared to show similar companies' fee schedules, the service provider redefines himself as a competent professional whose fees are competitive.

The VP of global ventures can correct the accusation of overreacting by saying, "The CEO is looking very carefully at this. We're both under the gun." Now she's no longer out of control; she's responding to legitimate pressure from the CEO.

How to Do It Without Insulting the Other Party Rosalind was a senior vice president in charge of human resources at an Illinois bank, where her skills were being underutilized. She began a new job search; however, her first interview started off disastrously. After bare-minimum introductions, the bank chairman fired questions at her about how she handled problem employees. When he ran out of steam, he complimented Rosalind on her people skills, but then said, "Unfortunately, the demands of a commercial bank require more expertise than just an ability to deal with difficult people."

Rosalind knew she had to correct his incomplete image of her and asked if she might respond. So she focused on her strongest bottom-line successes. She described how she had previously reduced teller mistakes from 82 percent to 15 percent. She explained how she had saved her bank $1.2 million over two years in long-term medical benefits by renegotiating contracts with insurance carriers. Her self-definition renewed the chairman's interest; from being dismissed she became desired.

We as women need to understand that every interview is a negotiation and get over the automatic assumption that it is our fault when an interview goes badly. The interviewer simply might not have a good idea of who you are or what you can do; résumés can communicate only so much. Correcting a wrong impression (as Rosalind did) brings the interviewer's assumptions about you into line with your real capabilities.

REDIRECT 5: BRING ATTENTION BACK TO THE ISSUE

Once a move is made, you can divert it to focus back on the problem itself. The marketing director might deploy a diverting redirect in a participative way to reengage her boss to talk salary: "I'd like to explore some other ideas with you."

How to Do It Without Harming the Relationship Here is an example of diverting with which many women will identify. Nadia was thinking about joining her father in their family-owned business. She knew her education and previous business experience would help the firm, where customer service, her specialty, had always been problematic. She could also lighten some of the burden her father had been carrying since her uncle's retirement. Because she was preparing to return to school for her M.B.A., Nadia knew the family business would give her the most time flexibility. Plus, she had just discovered she was pregnant.

"My family is Greek, very close, traditional, and warm," she said. "My father is a wonderful man but comes from the father-knows-best school. I had to be reassured he would not micromanage me." He worried about her juggling baby, school, and work.

When her father mentioned these concerns, Nadia diverted them by focusing on business issues: her needs for generous health benefits and a flexible schedule, his concerns about how her salary level might communicate favoritism to his valued longtime employees. Nadia continually moved the negotiation off her role as daughter and onto that of prospective employee.

They devised a win-win situation. Her father allowed her to work around her school schedule and do some work from home. In exchange, she accepted a cut in pay. To finish her degree, she would take an unpaid leave for a semester, but the company would reimburse her tuition. After the birth of her baby she would take the same maternity leave as other employees and also work at home. By diverting the conversation, Nadia's redirects shifted the focus from family relations and kept it on business.

The Case Against Counterattacking

It is better to redirect than to counterattack because being on the defensive is not a strong position. The other person's actions are governing you, preventing you from advocating for your own needs. It's a distraction and an energy drain; it makes it difficult to reclaim calm and authoritative leadership of the discussion. Denying, protesting, and giving as good as you get rarely change anyone's mind about you, and these behaviors often escalate tensions. Rhetoric heats, attitudes harden, exchanges slip into a cycle of "I am not" denials and "You are so" rebuttals. It triggers a battle of wills that fuels the urge to "put a woman in her place" in the sublevel negotiation.

Redirects are more effective than counterattacks because:

- They refute any suspicion that you may be weak or inexperienced, that you lack judgment or authority to make decisions, or that you are ruled by anger or emotion.
- They put the other party on notice that you will not stumble blindly into traps.
- They allow you to resist negative images that others try to impose upon you.
- They recast the way your opponent sees you.
- They allow you to actively resist, instead of passively reacting or enduring, without suffering negative consequences.
- They eliminate the need for hostile protests and elaborate explanations.
- They give you stamina to persist. Negotiators test each other all the time, either by outright challenges or by wearing down the other party.
- They let you keep control of negotiations, even when you are matched against tough dealmakers.
- They don't allow anyone to "put you in your place." You, and only you, define your place and your terms.

Choosing the Right Redirect

Choosing a redirect is the hardest part. Often a split-second decision must be made. If you are an intuitive woman, you have an advantage for quickly sensing what is needed. Otherwise, here are some handy guidelines for different situations:

- **You find yourself at a loss for words:** *Insert time and/or space.* Withhold answering for just a few seconds, or completely end the meeting and reconvene the next day.
- **You face testing moves in the early stages of a negotiation:** *Name and/or correct* to keep you from being pushed into a defensive position, and establish your control.
- **You face credibility challenges in the middle of a negotiation:** *Question* your opponent and ask for specifics and evidence to support

his claims about your image or credibility; this will often make him back down.

- **You face stalling or refusals toward the end of a negotiation:** *Divert* to move discussions toward a positive conclusion.

Implement a Multiple Redirect Strategy

Gloria Wallace used a full repertory of redirects when she took over a newly established sales department and had to negotiate internally for its fair share of clients. Gloria's new department was the brainchild of the vice president of sales. He wanted a separate sales group targeting start-ups in the growing nanotechnology field.

To get Gloria's department off the ground, $5 million in accounts had to be transferred from national sales. No problems surfaced in the planning meetings. Cooperatively, Gloria and Phil Browning, the manager of national sales, established reasonable criteria and a deadline for the transfer.

Gloria trusted Phil. Their personalities meshed, and they had a similar work ethic. She liked hearing his company war stories over coffee. When they went on sales calls or developed a presentation, they always learned a lot from each other.

Then the real negotiation began, and things changed. Because the department was new, with no track record and still building internal influence, Gloria was ripe for testing. Gloria's repeated phone calls to Phil prompted no action from him. The day before the annual sales meeting, when account assignments were distributed, Phil finally gave Gloria his list. This move made it clear that Phil thought he could force Gloria to make concessions and accept half the number of accounts she expected.

Time was not on Gloria's side. Her team was already grumbling about the account delays. When Gloria objected, Phil implied that she was being greedy and emotional. He came up with a revised list two weeks later, but it was filled with what Gloria suspected were dead accounts.

Is Phil the bad guy here? If you answer yes, you are, like many women, in denial about the motivations of your opponents and therefore forfeiting a lot of your power. The correct answer is no. He is doing what negotiators do—trying to maintain his advantage in the sublevel negotiation. To give up more accounts than is absolutely necessary is risky to his bottom line. His salespeople earn commissions from them; they don't want to give up that income. Also, one of those accounts might become the next nanotechnology superstar. When Phil tells Gloria her team is not ready for that many accounts, he is not playing dirty. He's trying to make sure the negotiation goes his way by conceding as few accounts as possible and giving a good reason for his actions. The following summarizes Phil's sublevel negotiation:

- He plays on Gloria's sympathy and her team's inexperience.
- He insinuates that she is not being cooperative when she challenges his list.
- He casts doubts on her abilities as a manager (whether she has the right temperament).
- He tries to position her as someone who takes things personally, who is too emotional and greedy to see the big picture.

At this point, Gloria has let Phil put her on the defensive, and she needs to redirect these moves. "It was clear to everyone that Phil didn't take me seriously," she recalls. "He thought it would be easy to overpower me or wear me down."

Gloria's strongest weapons for getting off the ropes and back into the game are to:

- Anticipate Phil's moves and *divert* the sympathy connection.
- *Label* his move of calling her team inexperienced and herself uncooperative and excitable to show him he is using ineffective negotiating strategies.
- Begin to share a few war stories of her own about her significant past sales successes to *correct* her image as an inexperienced manager.
- *Question* him to get him to list examples of her lack of cooperation, which, she believes, he will have a hard time enumerating.

Gloria's redirects have cut off Phil's momentum. Once he realizes his win-lose negotiation strategy is a waste of time, the sublevel negotiation returns to equal alignment. Working as equals, Gloria and Phil reach a solution that is fair to both.

The bottom line is that if you consistently and successfully redirect your opponents' sublevel moves, they will stop making moves, start doing the real work, and treat you with the respect you deserve.

Discover Your Negotiation Skills: Apply the Five Redirects

You can use this exercise to see how you would use the five redirects in an actual upcoming negotiation or, if one is not in your immediate future, in a past or imagined negotiation.

1. **Insert Time or Space:** How can you insert time or space into this particular situation? List at least three ways you can insert time and three ways you can insert space into the negotiation.

   Ways to insert time:

   _____

   _____

   _____

   _____

   Ways to insert space:

   _____

   _____

   _____

   _____

2. **Label the Move:** What can you say to demonstrate that you recognize the move your counterpart has just thrown at you? How can you say it gracefully?

   _____

   _____

3. ***Question the Move:*** What question can you ask that will throw the burden back on the mover? How can you ask the question to make it seem as if the move is puzzling or unprovoked?

4. ***Correct the Move:*** How can you correct the move in a gracious, nonaccusatory way? What evidence do you have to prove the claim is incorrect?

5. ***Divert Attention Back to the Issue:*** How can you divert the move to return the focus back onto the problem itself?

WINNING GAME PLANS: NEGOTIATING WITH POWER AND GRACE

Obstacles to Communication Between the Sexes

1. Conflicting styles
2. Conflicting ways to recognize achievement
3. To women, men are blind to their needs
4. To men, women are overly sensitive
5. To men, women ask too many questions
6. To women, men don't listen to them
7. Conflicting ways of expressing emotion
8. Both are insensitive to one another[1]

12

Gender Intelligence and Negotiation

When it comes to gender intelligence, it pays to be smart—big time. Deloitte & Touche USA (now Deloitte US), the big accounting firm, estimates it saves $190 million annually off the results of its gender intelligence training just by reducing its turnover of talented women.[1] That's nearly $1 billion saved by the firm in little over half a decade. So here, in dollars and sense (pun intended), we women can point to a measure of our value to corporate America. And that's at just one firm.

Deloitte & Touche did this based on modern neuroscience's explanation of the workings of female brains and how they complement the workings of the male brain, thereby harnessing rather than hindering these mental strengths in a business setting. As a result, Deloitte let women operate from their authentic selves, *rather than requiring them to act more like men.* In turn, women became more valued for the genuine abilities they bring to the table, and advancement opportunities opened up. No longer was it necessary to jump ship in order to move up the ranks, and Deloitte saved the substantial costs of replacing accomplished senior executive women.

What Neuroscience Teaches Us About Gender Intelligence in the Workplace

Research studies of past decades explored the external issues of male and female interactions in the workplace. How were women perceived? How did they operate—or not operate? The women who were studied functioned in business settings where men set the rules and imposed their ways of attaining goals on women. As a result, these studies quite accurately revealed what happens in a non-gender-intelligent environment.

For example, in 1974, studies done by Altemeyer and Jones concluded that a woman attempting to influence a group was more likely to be ignored than her male counterparts, and that men got more attention and had a greater effect on group members.[2] In 1983, studies revealed that in order to be considered as able as a man, a woman had to have solid proof that her performance was *superior* to his.[3] (Male competence was simply assumed.) Studies conducted by W. Wood and S. J. Karten in 1986 showed that people believed women to be less expert and knowledgeable than men (except in their traditional roles).[4] Even as late as 1999, research by L. L. Carli showed similar results to those of Wood and Karten.[5]

Many of these executive women are in the workforce today; they still have fresh memories of entering the negotiating room and being ignored, discounted, and disrespected. Is it any wonder that even among these accomplished female executives, there is uncertainty about how to handle the pitfalls of negotiations? A survey conducted in partnership by Women of Influence and Thomson Reuters titled "Women Leaders Breaking Through in Their Careers" revealed that fully three-quarters of the North American senior executive women surveyed claimed that their negotiation skills were "poor."[6]

Those women were right. They *were* poor *if* they were measured by how much like a man's they were. But women aren't like men; we have some unique advantages to offer. While men and women are equivalent in intellectual capacity, their brains produce different *kinds* of smarts.

Neuroscience, through new technologies like PET and SPECT (photo emission tomography and single-photon emission computed tomography) scans or MRIs, now allows us to see exactly which brain centers light up when men and women undertake certain tasks. The bottom line is that women receive more input from all our senses than men do, we process it through more parts of the brain than men do, and we express it more verbally. If you were a human resources executive looking for a good negotiator, wouldn't you want to hire someone with these abilities?

Not only that, but because women take in more information from all their senses than men do, they remember more information, and they remember it for longer, making them a valuable asset during post-negotiation briefings. This information also gets processed through a part of the female brain that deals with emotion, so the combination of fact and feeling input (which can be so critical to successfully closing a negotiation) is far more likely to come from a female negotiator.

Here is the (user-friendly) science behind these statements.

HIS BRAIN, HER BRAIN: THEIR IMPACT ON NEGOTIATIONS

Left Brain, Right Brain Scientists are learning more and more every day about the functions of the various parts of the brain. All human brains are structured essentially the same, with two sides, or hemispheres, but there are some unique differences in the blood flow and neural activity of men's and women's brains.

Hers: The various centers of verbal ability and emotions are found on both sides of the brain. In females, blood flow is greater to all these centers; thus, we have more ability to put our thoughts and emotions into words and to describe the inputs of our five senses. We talk in ways that invite pleasurable feedback to these emotional centers, for instance, ending our sentences with questions so people will respond. We apologize more and show appreciation more; we try to connect more.

His: The right side of the brain handles outer-world physical processing, such as seeing objects in space, the ability to rotate things in 3-D in our head, and the ability to understand how physical or mechanical objects work. In males, blood flow is more significant to the right brain than to the left. If these right-brain centers are not stimulated (for instance during a boring meeting), men become disengaged; some even fall asleep. Fidgeting, playing with pens or papers, and throwing wadded-up paper into wastebaskets are all ways men keep themselves consciously in the present (although to women it may look as though they're distracted or not interested). This brain orientation is also why men spread themselves out more physically; they are more engaged with the space they occupy. Although this is sometimes used as a power tactic, it is usually just an unconscious male brain trait. An intuitive gender-intelligent woman can tell the difference.

The Limbic System, the Amygdala, and the Cerebral Cortex The limbic system, located in the middle of your brain, is the area where you feel your feelings. Next time you feel a strong emotion, try to pinpoint where in your body you're feeling it and where it seems to be emanating from—this is a fun experiment. You will most likely end up deep inside the middle of your brain. Hello, limbic system!

Hers: Emotions don't just puddle in a woman's limbic system. In the female, there is a superhighway leading from the limbic system with an exit ramp straight into the cerebral cortex (that's up top), which makes thoughts and words. Our verbal centers are also more active than men's, and we have more words at our disposal. So, for example, angry women will talk a mean streak, until they've "gotten it all out." Verbal outpourings toward men are not a good strategy. Men cannot process words as fast as women can, so they interrupt or glaze over. They aren't being rude; they're pleading for us to slow down. If you're a woman whom men interrupt a lot, try using shorter sentences, backing away from emotions, and sticking to facts. If this doesn't modify their behavior, it's safe to assume they're disrespecting you (then it's time to call them on it, but not before).

His: The male brain can take many hours to process the same emotion-heavy experience that a woman can process in minutes. Men's stress emotions get directed not up to the cerebral cortex, but down by the amygdala, which is larger in males than females, to places in the brain that perceive the world in three dimensions and can devise strategies. Stress emotions also move more quickly to a man's aggression centers, creating fidgeting, pacing, gesticulating, and confrontational behavior. Consequently, men in stressful negotiations are louder and more physically expressive, which can seem intimidating to women.

The Cingulate Gyrus Sounds scary but it's not! The cingulate gyrus is located inside the limbic system. It takes life experiences and helps make connections to current input. It does a constant compare-and-contrast job. As we've discussed, a woman's limbic system, the emotional center, is more active than a man's.

Hers: Women get more input from the five senses: We compare the facial expressions around us to ones we've seen in the past, verbal tones, gestures, the messages clothing and grooming send, the composition of the negotiation team, conference table set-ups, and the like. This often leads men to brand women as "too sensitive." However, the information we are able to glean from this is valuable, and corporations are starting to harness female sensitivity about context and details of interaction for their bottom-line advantage. A word of caution: We need to control the time we spend on interpersonal dealings, which can overwhelm our task schedules.

His: Men are more comfortable sticking to facts they physically obtain. They excel at reading annual reports and financial statements and negotiating using such data. This is definitely a plus for a negotiator; such facts are hard to refute or negotiate away. But too often, a male negotiator will miss the more subtle signals put out by the opposition. He'll come away thinking he aced the agreement, and be surprised when the contract signing is delayed; his female associate will often know exactly why.

Gray Matter and White Matter Our brains are composed of two types of matter with separate functions. Gray matter performs focused tasks in single appropriate centers in the brain. The white matter is like the Internet—its job is to network and gather information from various brain centers.

Hers: Women are well-known multitaskers. Why? Because we have ten times more intellectual white matter than men. We can pay attention to multiple things at once, for example, a telephone call and what our toddler is getting into, or the many things that our boss wants us to do. We actively gather input from people on our team, routinely asking connecting questions like, "What else do we need to think about before we decide?" This dual-hemisphere, connection-creating brain function may trigger concern or confusion in a focused man, who thinks we're being dense because we "don't know the answer," or we're "going off on a tangent." Because a male brain is single focused, a man may require an explanation or even demonstration to understand the dual-hemisphere connection our brain just made.

His: Men are focused achievers. Why? Because they have almost six-and-a-half times more intellectual gray matter than we do. They work best with one input at a time and will rebuff distractions, sometimes angrily ("Not now, I'm busy!"). If you engage a man expecting him to multitask like you do, his frustration may come across as contempt or rejection; but his blood flow is not energizing the same brain centers as yours, and he simply needs to stay focused. You'll notice that men talk less than women do when they're actively working on a project; compare a woman who likes to talk to her family and/or watch TV while she cooks to a man who often needs to escape to his garage to work alone on a project. Men excel at focused tasks.

The Hippocampus The parts of female brains that handle emotions and sense memories have more pathways to the hippocampus than those of males do. It is the part of the brain that processes physical details, particularly as they affect ways to relate to someone.

"I really liked Ms. Carroll's office. Did you notice the aqua silk upholstery on her chairs, and that really sophisticated design of the wallpaper? Must have cost a fortune to decorate her office. Plus fresh flowers every day. We don't have to worry about this relationship; she's not going anywhere," says Janet to her co-presenter, Brent. "I noticed two things," he replies. "That impressive mahogany desk and the impressive deal we just signed and sealed on it." In this scenario, the woman is acting from her hippocampus.

Hers: Testing shows that women remember the details of interpersonal exchanges better than men do. The ability to relate to others can be crucial in developing business relationships through follow-up activities like entertainment or gift-giving. (If you can remember that a certain executive prefers a unique brand of Scotch or a particular type of European chocolates, it assists in cementing relationships down the road.) The hippocampus also assists in remembering things like facial expressions, or gestures of unconscious dissatisfaction.

His: Men are better at dealing with the immediate challenges presented by the physical world but less able to recall minute details of interactions. They will recall broad facts, and the more superficial parts of an interchange, particularly as they feed into their goal. After a meeting, men and women often give very different debriefings of what occurred. Gender intelligence directs that the information from both debriefings must be combined to get the whole picture.

HIS CHEMISTRY, HER CHEMISTRY: THEIR IMPACT ON NEGOTIATIONS

Now that you've seen that the science of the brain is approachable (and actually rather flattering), let's delve into how our different chemistries affect our negotiation strategies.

Hormonal Cycles Yes, they have cycles, too! Women have their well-known monthly cycles, but men have daily cycles of testosterone, and women who understand this can use it to their advantage. For example, never schedule an important negotiation with a man between 9 and 11 a.m. if you can help it. His testosterone surges during these hours, bringing with it increased aggression, ambition, and cockiness. He is more apt to push hard and be less apt to listen during this time of day. (But if you need something fixed or moved, this is the time to assign him the task. If he's your lawyer, it's a good time for closing arguments!) There is another similar testosterone surge in the early evening, which may be why it seems more difficult to win an argument with a husband coming home after work. Usually the best time to negotiate with a man—if you want him to listen more closely and be generally more agreeable and collaborative—is between 3 and 5 p.m., or after 8 p.m. (not a time you'd normally schedule a business meeting).

Neurochemical Differences Testosterone makes the man, as does vasopressin, the chemical that influences men to be territorial. While women also secrete these neurochemicals, men definitely secrete more; in the case of testosterone, up to twenty times more. Women secrete more serotonin (an impulse-calming chemical) and oxytocin (a bonding chemical) than men do. When you describe someone as being "drunk with love," that person's body is actually in a state where it is producing high amounts of oxytocin. None of these chemicals is better or more important than the others; they just offer distinct advantages when applied to the right business demands. Vasopressin assists men in establishing negotiation boundaries; serotonin gives women the desire to jump in and calm things down during heated exchanges. Oxytocin helps a woman create and sustain lasting business relationships and partnerships.

Brain Chemistry and Competition Styles While men are thought of as the more competitive sex, constantly testing one another's strength and skills, it would be a mistake to think women are not competitive. Both sexes are competitive, but they act out this trait in different arenas. Testosterone and vasopressin drive males to compete over territory, increase their aggression levels, and challenge others physically or spatially. Women compete verbally over the status and quality of relationships. Their competition, too, is driven by testosterone, but, because they excrete less of this hormone, their competitive urges are not acted out in as physical a manner as men's. Women's competitive verbal exchanges are laced with subtleties, and over-layered with multiple meanings. With more words at our disposal, and more sense memories through which to communicate, we become masters at verbal one-upmanship. A gender-intelligent male-female negotiating team would therefore be formidable indeed!

Gender Intelligence in Practice

So what does all this science and chemistry mean at work?

It's difficult for women to make verbal and relational connections with men who are in competitive and/or aggressive modes. It is uncomfortable for either sex to move too much beyond their natural brain chemistry. Gender intelligence simply provides tools for effective communications when needed in a business setting. It is not about either sex changing but rather expanding awareness to take advantage of each other's strengths and minimize misunderstandings.

Knowing that puzzling behaviors are physiologically based, not the result of hate or contempt, should broaden the career potential for thousands of talented men and women. For example, when forming negotiating teams, gender intelligence means making sure that *all* human strengths are brought to bear. Trained mixed-gender teams will produce more deals that are successfully closed. Team composition can be engineered in the preplanning stage by strategically countering the strengths of the other team's leader and members. Pairing gender-intelligent facts-and-figures strategists with verbal-emotive specialists will prevent numerous missteps and lead more negotiations to successful conclusions.

The idea of co-gender leadership is now being explored within more progressive circles of big business. The co-gender model is nothing new; there are thousands of mom-and-pop operations throughout the United States that the Fortune 500 can study to learn best practices. Companies that prefer to remain with a single-leader model could optimize the role of the CEO by assigning those people Michael Gurian and Barbara Annis call "bridge brains"—the one in seven men and one in five women who share some of both male and female brain characteristics.[7]

In this chapter, I've mapped out a number of the most significant brain differences between men and women and demonstrated that women not only have a place at the negotiating table, but going forward will be critical to the success of every corporation globally. Women who are encouraged to operate authentically (as opposed to being forced to mimic men) provide significant, bottom line–enhancing advantages to those companies able to tap gender intelligence for the profit center it truly is. Firms that become early adopters of gender intelligence will enjoy a substantial strategic advantage during the first half of this century. As women stay with their companies longer, they will reap the benefits of advancement in both position and compensation.

The glass ceiling is cracking, at last.

Discover Your Gender Intelligence: Leadership

The questions in the following exercise will help you determine how keen your gender intelligence is. Circle your answers, and then compare them to those in the answer key on page 169.

GENDER LEADERSHIP				
1. You have submitted your anticipated action plan to your team members. This plan requires them to make some decisions. Who do you think would make a faster decision, a male or a female team member?	Male team member	Female team member		
2. A few days after presenting your initial proposal/action plan, you are meeting with a female team member. You find her to be more talkative during this meeting than at the presentation. Is she more likely to be on board with your plan?	Yes	No		
3. You're about to sit down for a meeting with a male team member after submitting your desired plan. The proposed changes are much more than he expected. Is he more likely to be more or less talkative during this meeting?	More talkative	Less talkative	The same	
4. When dealing with a male team member, is it better to show respect or appreciation for him?	Show respect	Show appreciation		
5. During the early stages of a relationship with a new team member you made a "casual commitment." Who is more likely to hold your feet to the fire to keep your commitment, a male team member or a female team member?	Male team member	Female team member	Both genders	Neither gender

6. When a female team member or coworker is stressed about a problem, is she more likely to shut her door and work out the problem or walk around the office talking to coworkers?	Shut her door	Walk around talking		
7. To which gender team member would you not boast or self-promote?	Male team member	Female team member	Both genders	Neither gender
8. When meeting with which team member for the first time should you make sure you bond well prior to starting your business "pitch"?	Male team member	Female team member	Both genders	Neither gender
9. If there is an issue, for which gender team member would you make sure you provide a quick solution?	Male team member	Female team member	Both genders	Neither gender
10. With which gender team member do you make sure to explain how the proposed plans will impact that person (meaning that in addition to presenting the plan, you explain the anticipated outcome)?	Male team member	Female team member	Both genders	Neither gender
11. With which gender team member do you make sure you are brief and come to the point quickly?	Male team member	Female team member	Both genders	Neither gender
12. For which gender team member would you most need to make sure that you listen with 100 percent attention?	Male team member	Female team member	Both genders	Neither gender
13. For which gender team member are your credentials more likely to make the person want to follow you?	Male team member	Female team member	Both genders	Neither gender
14. For which gender team member would you most need to make sure you are very clear in your message and that you get to the point?	Male team member	Female team member	Both genders	Neither gender

15. As a leader you will often be called upon to provide solutions to problems of team members. For which gender team member would you most need to make sure you do not rush in with a solution even if you have one ready (meaning that you pause before presenting your solution)?	Male team member	Female team member	Both genders	Neither gender
16. Which gender team member most needs space to think about any new plan you may want the person to be part of (meaning that you need to leave him or her alone to think it through)?	Male team member	Female team member	Both genders	Neither gender
17. Which gender team member would most appreciate you showing him or her how to be happier at work?	Male team member	Female team member	Both genders	Neither gender
18. When dealing with which gender team member do you bond better by showing how your plans will meet a specific need?	Male team member	Female team member	Both genders	Neither gender
19. To which gender team member is it most important to demonstrate extensive business knowledge?	Male team member	Female team member	Both genders	Neither gender
20. Which gender team member needs the most time to think something through and not be rushed to a decision?	Male team member	Female team member	Both genders	Neither gender
21. For which gender team member would you most need to have all the answers ready?	Male team member	Female team member	Both genders	Neither gender
22. For which gender team member would you most need to focus on showing the person how to be successful at the job?	Male team member	Female team member	Both genders	Neither gender

23. For which gender team member would you most need to make sure you hold back on giving all the answers and instead offer to do research and get back to the person on at least some questions? (Strange as it may sound, one gender will not like it if you have all the answers to questions at the tip of your tongue.)	Male team member	Female team member		
24. When dealing with a female team member is it better to show respect toward her or show appreciation for her?	Show respect	Show appreciation		

ANSWER KEY		
1. Male team member	9. Male team member	17. Female team member
2. No	10. Female team member	18. Male team member
3. Less talkative	11. Male team member	19. Male team member
4. Show respect	12. Female team member	20. Female team member
5. Female team member	13. Male team member	21. Male team member
6. Walk around talking	14. Male team member	22. Female team member
7. Female team member	15. Female team member	23. Female team member
8. Female team member	16. Male team member	24. Show appreciation

13

How, When, and Why to Make Concessions

Making concessions advantageously during negotiation is a real art. But it is also a science, and there are rules that will up your game. In this chapter, we will look at the art of conceding from four vantage points: (1) the concessions we make to ourselves, (2) the concessions we make to others, (3) the concessions we should not make at all, and (4) the concessions we accept. We'll conclude the chapter with some tips about ways to make the other side offer those acceptable concessions.

Unnecessary Concessions: Those You Make to Yourself

There is a danger zone during prenegotiation planning. It's the time when we start to formulate what we can "realistically" expect to get. As women, we are raised to be self-sacrificing; this is a good trait for mothers, but a bad one for business executives. Downplaying our needs so our children, spouses, friends, or the causes we believe in can have better opportunities or outcomes leaves us unprepared for negotiating favorable business terms. Our view of "realistic" and a man's may be quite different going into a negotiation.

But to whom are we conceding when we decide what's "realistic" to want or expect from a negotiation? It's just us alone inside our heads. If you've gotten this far in the book, it's likely you have made some major changes, so here's a few more. If you are currently in a negotiation, go to what you think is "realistic," then expand it by 100 percent. If you are not in that situation right now, imagine one or think back on an earlier one and do the same thing. It's OK to have an ambitious starting point.

You may think you know what's possible to achieve in a negotiation, but no one really does (not even veteran negotiators). This is something that has to be tested, time and again, before you can reasonably rely on instinct. Ask others what they would expect in a particular negotiation, and you'll get widely varying views. In order to win, you have to know what "win" means—to you. Without this as your starting point, creating a "win-win" scenario is impossible. So anchor yourself with this expectation: "Winning" means getting *more* than you expected.

I know you think you have to make concessions in order to avoid hostility and confrontation. You think if you ask for less, and accept less, then everyone will be happy (and if everyone is happy, then you will be, too). Wrong. This is a myth that you need to stop believing, starting now. You won't be happy, and neither will your boss! Asking for less and accepting less not only *does not prevent* hostility and confrontation, it actually may *encourage* it if your opponent sees that you'll settle for less.

There's another area where we often concede in our own minds, and that is when the other side doesn't hold up its end of the bargain, but we feel obliged to hold up ours anyway as a matter of integrity. The fact is we're *not* obligated to be our opponents' role model. They are adults. If they renege without cause or compensation, walk away from the deal. Don't do business with them again. You've lost a little and can move on to better arrangements; they'll have lost a lot. They won't be able to do business with you again, and likely they'll keep narrowing their sphere of influence by repeating this behavior until it impacts their bottom-line ability to do business at all. You don't need to go down with someone else's ship.

Women in their personal lives are rewarded for being flexible. Flexibility to meet the needs of children, spouses, family members, and the community is something that underpins civilized life. Flexibility is necessary in negotiation, but often not rewarded. This is especially true when we are too flexible too early. Retreating from our demands quickly sends the message that there may be more "wiggle room." Instead of procuring our counterparts' approval, we invite their escalated demands; they will then test us just to see how far we will bend. So don't concede to the "obligation" of being flexible in your own head first. Flexibility should be introduced slowly, from a position of strength and strategy. And it should always be rewarded.

When it comes to negotiating raises, bonuses, and perks, women often mentally concede their own worth before they ever start. Downplaying our worth and accomplishments is part of how we as women learn to form relationships—look for commonality, not distinction. We've all seen how women who brag experience backlash, with others—men and women—trying to "cut them down to size." It becomes a natural mental tendency for women to be humble and self-effacing, hoping that others will notice our fine work and reward it. But that's rarely how it works in business. Somewhere in our secret selves, we all know our real worth. Once we acknowledge and accept it in ourselves, we can begin building a rational, strategic case for getting the compensation we deserve for our efforts. Men who watch women undersell themselves are constantly mystified by why we do this, but they are more than willing to profit from it.

We often mentally concede to the idea of making a goodwill gesture (especially at the beginning of a negotiation) to set the tone. We can then emotionally reward ourselves for being noble and wait for the other party to reciprocate. Doing this frequently causes us to leave the bargaining table dissatisfied: "I made a goodwill gesture to them, but they didn't reciprocate." We may find that feeling noble is sufficient reward, or we may not. If we don't, then we need to take responsibility for making a concession that wasn't rewarded, and learn not to do so again.

A tough concession to ask women to rethink is the one where we tell ourselves we have to be fair. If the other party comes down by $100, then we think it's fair to go up $100. If they offer to "split the difference," we feel obligated to say yes because that's the "fair" and "right" thing to do. I'm telling you not to allow yourself to succumb to these pressures. If you have something of greater value than what the other party is offering to pay, the only fair thing to do is stand your ground. You must be fair to yourself first. If you are, you will teach others how to treat you, create reasonable boundaries, and increase your self-worth. Being fair does not apply just to how you treat others. Do not concede "fairness" to everyone else first and yourself last.

On the personal level, an internal concession women often make unnecessarily is deciding what we do and do not deserve. There are so many things affecting us when it comes to our beliefs about what we deserve—family values, traumatic incidents, societal messages, religious beliefs—that our self-worth, even legitimate needs, can get buried under them all. This is where practicing the art of negotiation can actually provide a healing experience. Go for the gold; if you get it, work on feeling you deserve it. Going for the gold *only* if you feel you deserve it can leave you stalled at the starting line.

Necessary Concessions: Those You Make to Others

The fact is you will make concessions to your counterpart. Concessions move negotiations forward, but you must make them correctly. Never, and I mean never, concede without getting something of equivalent value in return. Defining what equivalent value means is up to you, but don't be self-sacrificing here! You may trade tit-for-tat: a $200 price adjustment for $200 off delivery costs. You may trade tangibles for intangibles: goods for services; dinner at an expensive restaurant in exchange for someone making a speech at your club's annual meeting; a used computer in exchange for a teacher's gratitude and smile. It doesn't matter what it is, but it matters very much that it is an equal exchange. Making concessions in exchange for something of equal value is a revolutionary thought in many women's minds because of our cultural conditioning toward self-sacrifice.

So many women have doomed themselves to failure in negotiations, both professional and personal, by thinking that they will please others, and ultimately be offered what they want, by making concessions. This generosity often carries unspoken expectations that are ignored and unfulfilled. *Pleasing by conceding is not the way to get what you want* in a business negotiation. It sets you up to be manipulated into doing it again and again. After making what seem like expected concessions, many women feel confused, betrayed, and used when the other side doesn't spontaneously offer concessions in kind. Both personal and professional concessions need to be given only with clearly negotiated rewards; even if you think it's obvious, the other side probably doesn't understand what's important to you, so tell them.

We may make the mistake of thinking that a quick concession will generate goodwill, but it does not. It makes the other party think there's more to be gained because you conceded so quickly. They'll just keep trying to get more. An important rule of thumb: *Try never to make the first concession.* If you are negotiating with someone who also holds this philosophy, then talks may stall early. In this case, make a concession to get things moving, but make it a small, minor (and rewarded) one. *The concessions the other side has to work hard for are the ones they most value.*

Here are some tactics for how to make concessions work in your favor.

- **Don't move away from your original demand too quickly.** Moving away in itself is a concession, and often goes unrewarded. Of course you need to leave room to negotiate, but start with a high, yet reasonable, demand. Legitimize what you're asking for in any way you can—facts, figures, morality, legality—then step back and wait for a response. Learn all you can about what's really important to the other party before making a counterproposal; *never think you know what they want until they tell you.* You might give away too much money if you assume wrongly that money is their top priority.
- **Ask your counterparts to criticize your proposed list of demands.** You'll learn a lot about what's truly important to them, perhaps more than they would have revealed otherwise.
- **Make big concessions at the beginning of a negotiation.** Concessions should get smaller and smaller as negotiations go on. If you keep conceding the same amount (or more) of money, goods, services, or other desirables each time, the other side has no idea where your true price is so they'll keep pushing you. *Put the brakes on their demands—make your concessions more conservative each time.*
- **Don't let the other side manipulate you with silence.** If they look at you stony-faced, you'll be sorely tempted to fill that silence with concessions. *Don't.* Greet their silence with your own patient, unruf-

fled silence. Sit back, fold your hands, look out the window, and wait. Make silence your strength, not your weakness.

- **Never concede without getting something equivalent in return; describe fully and accurately what you want for your concession.** "I'll pay your full $1,500 consulting fee for the proposed training program, if you throw in free materials for all the attendees plus your three-hour advanced training session for our seven key executives. Deal?" Ask for more than you think you can get and know what you'll minimally settle for.

   It's one thing to ask for equivalent value for concessions you make. It's another thing to actually get it. You won't always have the luxury of negotiating with people who want to establish a long-term relationship with you. How do you protect yourself when you know they're out to get all they can by any means?

- **Make your concessions contingent on their payment or performance.** You may become tempted to use this tactic in all negotiations, but remember that this approach interferes with the building of trust and is not appropriate where you want to build long-term relationships, professionally or personally. But if you feel your goodwill is being exploited or manipulated, start placing contingencies on everything you agree to. "We can provide a two-month turnaround only if you agree to purchase our higher-priced, quick-install appliances."

- **Keep a written record of each concession you make as you go.** If possible, get the other party to initial each so there's no misunderstanding later. Toward the end of the negotiation, the sheer volume of concessions you've already made can be used as a bargaining chip in itself. In writing, your list of concessions will be difficult to refute or downplay.

- **Stall before conceding.** It's easy to get overwhelmed by the number of concessions the other side asks you to make. If you are under pressure to make a deal, the temptation may be to agree to the concessions en masse just to move on, especially if they all seem minor. However, it's better to create some time to consider what your opponents are asking for and how much needs to be demanded in return.

If you concede too soon, the other side will not value what you've given them as much as if you make them wait for it. So, let them cool their heels while you go do some research about how much it actually costs your company to provide free delivery, or what will happen to your warehouse capacity (in dollars per square foot) if you agree to store their inventory on-site. The other side will value a concession more if they have to wait an hour to get it than if they have to wait five minutes.

- **Keep several lists of possible concessions in mind.** This is in case what you offer holds little value to the other side, or they are unable to meet your demands. If the other side doesn't care about your double warranty program, then offer free replacement or free delivery. Thinking up concessions on the spot, under pressure, is tough; creative and satisfying deals require forethought as well as thinking on your feet.

The No-Fly Zone: Concessions You Should Never Make

We women have been trained to make concessions in ways that harm us in the business setting. Unless we've been lucky enough to pick up some pointers from business-oriented relatives at the dinner table, we've mostly learned how concessions can be used to make other people like us on a personal level. This will hold you back in the business arena.

Following are some things you should never do in a negotiation:

- **Never open with the minimum you will accept.** Do not concede your bottom line at the opening gate under the guise of "simply being honest." You must leave room to negotiate, if for no other reason than to feel out what's truly important to your counterpart. "Wiggle room" is not dishonest; it facilitates the "getting to know you" portion of relationship-building.
- **Never tell the other party how much you want what they have.** You are conceding a considerable amount of your power to them without gaining back anything equivalent. This allows them to offer

you less. Classic example: gushing over a house you're touring with a real estate agent; it will keep the price high. Telling a prospective boss how badly you want the job for which you are interviewing will hold down your salary offer. Show enthusiasm for the position, of course, but ask for 24 hours to "think over" the offer, even if you know privately that you're going to accept. Be sure to ask if there's any room for negotiating the salary offer before you leave.

- **Do not make big concessions quickly.** Yes, you have to make your bigger ones at the beginning, but make your opponent wait. Listen and learn before giving anything away. Then go slowly, bit by bit. Make them work (and pay!) for everything they get.

- **Do not make large concessions when you are under pressure to "get the deal done."** You will send the wrong message about what you're really willing to give to the other party, and they'll adopt a strategy of holding out for more. This slows things down rather than speeding them up. It's possible that if you're under pressure, so are they, so feel your way through the mutually rewarding concessions that are necessary to create a timely win-win resolution. Go slow to go fast.

- **Under no circumstances concede to your own raw emotions.** It's very tempting to try to get even with someone who has wronged you. But you'll be conceding power and authority with no equivalent return. They say "revenge is a dish best served cold"; nowhere is that more true than in a negotiation. Chill; strategize; channel strong emotion into creating powerful positions.

- **Slow down when you feel forced to accept something you don't want.** Do not concede to anything unacceptable or uncomfortable until you've done some homework on possible alternatives. If someone throws you an unanticipated demand at the table, call a time-out, do your homework, and explore other options. Make the other party wait for your concession, which with each passing minute becomes more valuable.

- **Don't become putty in anyone's hands.** You may find yourself one day across the table from someone famous, beautiful, or otherwise awe-inspiring. You may have to negotiate with the hottest man you ever saw walk the surface of the planet. Don't make concessions because you're star-struck. Make a conscious decision to rein it in.

- **Never let the other party define the reward for a concession you've made.** You and you alone know what is truly valuable to you. Don't wait for offers. Make requests and demands.
- **Here's a biggie: Make no concession that will cause resentment to fester between you and those with whom you are negotiating.** When you do this, you may feel self-righteous in the moment, but festering resentments build into unresolved circular arguments and damaging blowups. Walk away from a negotiation and strategize, rather than concede to anything that can have this result. Always invest in the win-win when it comes to long-term relationships like partnerships or with clients of long-standing.

Maximize the Concessions You Accept:
Getting Others to Concede to You

Inevitably, when women start to negotiate more effectively, they are shocked at what they can get, and chagrined by what they've previously left on the table. It's time to make up for that! Here are some strategies you can use:

- **Flinch or blink with surprise at the other side's initial offer.** This modifies their expectations of what they might ultimately extract from you.
- **Meet their offer with silence, prolonged if necessary.** Concessions often flow to fill the gap.
- **If you are offered something that is less valuable than what you've offered, challenge it.** Don't think that's all you're going to get.
- **Ask for stuff.** Get your counterpart to sweeten a deal—favorable payment terms (no interest, longer time), free delivery/set-up/training/service, on-site repairs, free add-ons, guaranteed trade-in price,

removal of current equipment or help in selling it, discounted upgrades in the future, money-back guarantees. Strategize about what might make life easier for you or your company—specification changes, schedule modifications, delivery terms.

Discover Your Personal Values: Testing Your Beliefs Under Pressure

Making concessions creates pressure. You have to decide what you're willing to give up, and how you're going to hold fast for what you want. These situations can put pressure on your values (as anyone who has ever seen the movie *Sophie's Choice* can understand).

Call to mind any situation in which your values were tested under pressure in a negotiation or elsewhere. Then answer the following:

1. What resources did I call upon under this pressure?
2. To what extent did I deviate from my values?
3. What would I do differently if I had it to do all over again?

14

Negotiating with the "Big Boys"

"Big boys" is a term that elicits a reaction. It brings up memories of competition on the playground; the power, sometimes abused, of older siblings or classmates; and the win-at-any-cost manipulations of male business moguls. The male brain is wired to be competitive, to solve problems that get in the way of winning; it is less likely to factor in emotions, long-term relationship building, or creatively crafting win-win scenarios. But some women are quite capable of engaging in this "big boy" negotiation style as well. So going forward the term "big boy" will refer to any big player, male or female, who engages in advanced (or over-the-line) power moves. Without a strong grounding in negotiation techniques, you are an easy mark for the "big boys."

The previous chapters were dedicated to giving you that grounding. In them I outlined how to intensively prepare for an upcoming negotiation, and I provided many at-the-table tools for interpersonal success. I hope you've absorbed that information, started to use it in your daily life, and made it your own. If so, you are ready for this chapter; if not, I suggest you review the earlier chapters until you feel comfortable with the techniques and then proceed.

In their article, "3-D Negotiation/Playing the Whole Game," David A. Lax and James K. Sebenius discuss a third dimension of negotiating: "Savvy

3-D negotiators work behind the scenes, away from the table, both before and during negotiations to set (and reset) the bargaining table. They make sure that all the right parties are approached in the right order to deal with the right issues at the right time."[1]

"Big boys" are very skilled in using this third dimension, which requires thinking big. Here, you're not just trying to psych out your counterparts, or sharpen your verbal strengths to exploit advantage and achieve your goals, you're thinking strategically and asking yourself questions like, "Who do I need to get on board first, second, and third so number four (my most desired partner) can't help but join?" "How else can we make the pie bigger for everyone, especially me?"

At the "big boy" level, deals may involve millions, even billions, of dollars. Getting it right can have huge impacts in terms of dollars and people's lives. At this level, the art of the win-win really contributes to the quality of life, and win-lose can mean fabulous profits for some and ruined lives for others.

Negotiation Mapping Model

I created the Negotiation Mapping Model as a planning tool to help you operate at this "huge outcome" level. Here are its seven components; not every negotiation will require that you use each one.

1. **Backwards Mapping:** Determine the things and the order in which they have to happen for you to meet your objective.
2. **All Party Listing:** Identify participants in terms of existing and potential relationships.
3. **Value Assessment:** Identify what's in it for your counterparts. Ask yourself why they should do business with you and why you rather than your competitor.
4. **Management of Emotions in High-Stakes Negotiations:** Figure out how not to get bogged down in heated exchanges and diversions from the task at hand when facing complex emotional issues. Ask yourself questions about your counterparts' priorities and pressures; demonstrate your desire to give them what they want as

long as you get everything you want, too. Show by words and deeds a desire to add value for all parties involved.

5. **Barriers Audit:** Identify potential obstacles; consider how to manage unanticipated hurdles; and plan ways to neutralize or navigate them.

6. **Plan Creation:** This is where you pull it all together. Get grounded in as many possible issues and concerns of the other party as you can. Get as much background information on all relevant players as you can. Research, strategize, and plan concessions and useful moves. Determine how you will cover your back, if necessary.

7. **Delivery on the Opportunity:** Do future planning so that you can move in quickly with a show of strength if you win the opportunity you're negotiating for. Line up resources and allies now so you can hit the ground running.

I will demonstrate the Negotiation Mapping Model, drawing on key elements of the Harvard Business School's two reports on Sarah Talley and her company, Frey Farms Produce.[2]

BACKWARDS MAPPING

Sarah Talley's family owned and operated Frey Farms Produce in Keenes, Illinois, which acted as a hub for delivering fresh fruits and vegetables to local Midwest grocery stores. The farm was particularly well known for pumpkins and watermelons, commodities with seasonal upswings due to brief but intense holiday demands. Taking the reins at an early age, 19-year-old president Sarah negotiated a deal to supply these items, plus fall ornamentals, to Walmart just as the retail giant was entering the grocery supply business.

By backwards mapping at this stage Sarah was able to overcome several hurdles. She recognized that Walmart's focus on providing the lowest prices was the key to unlocking the business. She already had the contacts in place to source cheaply and quickly from local and regional growers, but some of her competitors were international conglomerates with deeper pockets that could buy newer technology and more influence. She also knew she had to address the issue of her age, and perhaps gender, in order to convince Walmart to deal with her.

Sarah realized that her competitors' all-expenses-paid lunches and field tours weren't going to communicate low-priced efficiency to some of the world's most experienced and savvy buyers. In her initial interactions with these buyers, she also found that Walmart's internal commitment to its "everyday low prices (EDLP)" superseded any concerns about her age and gender. If she convinced them she could deliver high-quality, locally grown produce within their price point and freshness parameters, she would win a chunk of business that would cement the future of Frey Farms. She addressed all the concerns that Walmart wanted to hear, and her company got the nod. It was Frey Farms' first step up the corporate partnership ladder.

ALL PARTY LISTING

By her mid-twenties, Sarah had ascended to CEO of Frey Farms Produce, and had done business successfully with Walmart on the local level, supplying through some of Walmart's larger co-managers for a number of seasons. She now had a new goal: to gain co-management status with Walmart for Frey Farms. Sarah explains, "Co-management is where suppliers jointly manage the business, sharing the responsibility of meeting goals, meeting margin, sales, inventory levels, etc."[3] It is a strong relationship, and one not easily awarded by Walmart.

To negotiate this status meant having to build credibility at Walmart's headquarters. Who could make the "big boys" listen to the Frey Farms story? Sarah needed to talk to the right people in the right order at the right times.

Sarah aligned herself again with Walmart's internal culture and EDLP focus. Forced by Walmart, as she now was, to supply through its existing mega-sized co-managers, the infrastructure costs imposed by those middlemen would have to be added to the cost of Sarah's product. She began quantifying these costs to the regional Walmart buyers, who saw her logic and supported her bid for co-management status to the buying team at the local home office. The local buying team, in turn, introduced her to regional buyers, who helped her gain access to the agricultural product category managers at headquarters. Here, she learned that the pressures of fast growth had blinded the category managers to the financial drawbacks of co-managing only with mega-suppliers.

Sarah had talked to the right people in the right order at the right times.

VALUE ASSESSMENT

Now, Sarah had to address Walmart's fundamental questions: (1) What was in it for the company to elevate Frey Farms to co-management status? (2) Why go with Frey rather than a competitor or staying with the mega-suppliers? (3) Did Frey Farms have the required capabilities?

Sarah worked hard to learn Walmart's culture and internal language. She related to Walmart, not as an anonymous big-box store but as a group of people with a culture and language all their own who were committed to providing low prices to their customers and who treated their suppliers and co-managers fairly. Sarah learned this, respected it, and worked within this framework, actually going further than any of the other potential suppliers. She was determined to prove to Walmart that her commitment to creating low prices and appreciation of its corporate culture was just as strong as the company's own.

Proving this was key to achieving co-management status. So while her "big boy" competitors were financing $12,000 tractors, Frey Farms was purchasing used school buses for $1,500 to transport melons. Her buses were able to travel at 50 miles per hour to market, substantially faster than the more expensive tractors hauling wagons. This was a brilliant way to find "new money" and position Frey Farms as a problem-solving partner.

MANAGEMENT OF EMOTIONS IN HIGH-STAKES NEGOTIATIONS

Negotiating supplier prices with Walmart for holiday produce like watermelons and pumpkins can be very stressful. Walmart has many options when selecting suppliers and is not generally willing to back off on its price demands. When factors like weather, disease, or pests affect crop levels, the pressure typically is on the supplier to shave its income.

Therefore, when it came time to negotiate price, Sarah began by asking questions. She *quizzed* Walmart's buyers on their assessments of crop conditions, distribution, and overall cost of goods, *guiding* them to arrive at her preferred answers. She *kept the focus* on the greater goals of what was right for both Frey Farms and Walmart working in partnership. If partnership tensions do erupt, they are addressed immediately and not allowed to fester.

At her company, she does not allow any question to be debated for more than five minutes; this prevents stalling tactics and emotional escalation.

BARRIERS AUDIT

Sarah correctly identified two barriers to achieving co-management status: (1) Walmart was in a growth mode and (2) the decision-makers at headquarters had little time to assess what was happening in the trenches, even though it was taking the company away from its stated goals. Sarah had to attract their attention. Because she had a limited time in which to meet with the higher-ups, she had to plan persuasive arguments that would quickly create credibility for herself and her company.

PLAN CREATION

Sarah studied the chain of command and worked her way up it starting with people she knew and had already worked with. The core of her plan was to leverage Walmart's commitment to low prices by showing how achieving her goal of co-management fed directly into the retailer's commitment. She researched, quantified, and actively demonstrated the price disadvantages that would result if Frey Farms was forced to supply Walmart through mega-sized co-managers. Then she communicated in dollars and cents exactly how these costs would be shaved if Frey dealt directly with Walmart as a co-manager.

Sarah did not meet to negotiate with Walmart only once; there were many small negotiating sessions. Each time, she moved her way up the corporate ladder. She framed her desires as opportunities for Walmart to meet its own goals of low pricing and superior supplier relationships. She delivered her message in Walmart's own unique, acronym-laced language, using terms like "EDLP" (everyday low prices). Because she had created a concrete plan for achieving the lowest possible prices and was able to communicate it by "talking their talk," the "big boys" at headquarters awarded her co-management status. In 2003 Frey Farms, led by its 26-year-old CEO, received Walmart's "Co-managed Supplier of the Year" award.

DELIVERING ON THE OPPORTUNITY

Once you win, you have to deliver. Before her final pitch to win co-management status, Sarah studied the experiences of other Walmart co-managed companies. She absorbed Walmart's expectations and developed an execution strategy.

Today, Sarah employs a replenishment analyst and a business analyst to act as liaisons with Walmart's buyers and distribution centers. The replenishment analyst handles the inventory and the business analyst assesses sales targets and negotiated margins.

Know Your Stuff; Stand Your Ground

One of Sarah Talley's strengths, even from an early age, was going into negotiations with confidence. She would not back down, or "blink," during high-pressure price negotiations. It's not that she was stubborn or emotionally invested; she simply knew her stuff and stood her ground.

When you get the opportunity to deal with the "big boys," knowing your stuff is required, but standing your ground takes courage and determination. A well-known negotiation acronym we haven't yet discussed is BATNA; it stands for "Best Alternative to Negotiated Agreement." This means if the "big boys" force you into an untenable position, you should ask yourself:

- What will it cost you to walk away? Frey Farms' answer was an "enormous growth opportunity."
- Will your company stay in business? Frey Farms Produce could answer "yes."
- Will it cost you your career? Frey Farms Produce and Sarah Talley could answer "no." The strength to stand your ground comes from knowing (1) what will happen if you walk away, and (2) that you can handle it. If you aren't clear about your BATNA, you'll be a candidate for caving in to unfavorable terms—you'll "blink."

Standing your ground is how you gain the "big boys'" respect. Successful negotiators never overdepend on one source of business or income. If any one client constitutes more than 20 percent of your total business revenue, you're not ready to do business with that client. If they constitute more than 50 percent of your revenue, you'll be "blinking" at every demand they make.

Discover Your Negotiation Skills:
High-Stakes Negotiations

Negotiating with the "big boys" requires more examination during the planning stage than other negotiations because the stakes are so much greater. Use the worksheet to practice planning a high-stakes negotiation.

NEGOTIATION MAPPING MODEL EXERCISE

Instructions: "High-stakes" negotiations must be examined in more depth during the planning stage. Use the worksheet on page 188 to practice planning a high-stakes negotiation.

	PLAN CREATION
BACKWARDS MAPPING What has to happen for me to get what I want?	
ALL PARTY LISTING Identify all parties involved.	
VALUE ASSESSMENT What's in it for them?	
MANAGEMENT OF EMOTIONS How can I keep my focus on the greater goal if my emotions get triggered?	
BARRIERS AUDIT What can get in the way? How can I neutralize it?	

15

Negotiate Your Way
to Leadership Success

If your ambition is to be on your company's leadership track (or you're already there), I want to make sure you've given adequate thought to your motivation. Too often, we think our bosses have it easier than we do. They've already achieved status and respect, we think. Others are doing the work that they're overseeing. It seems cushy to those of us down in the trenches paying our dues.

Behind the curtain, it all has to do with negotiation skills. Leaders maneuver every day to strengthen their positions, enhance their status, and garner resources—all in pursuit of making things happen by persuading teams of people to work their hardest and best.

Leadership and negotiation skills are almost interchangeable descriptions of the same activity. Poor negotiators never make it to the executive suite, because they don't know which battles to fight and which demand strategic retreat and regrouping. And they think they have to fight every battle themselves. At best, this will land you squarely in lower middle management, watching others leapfrog ahead of you.

Critical Points to Hit When Negotiating
for a New Position

You've decided that you're up for the challenge of leadership and have made a study of what's required. Now you're at a critical crossroads. The phrase "hit the ground running" is no longer a theory; it's something you'll be doing in the next two weeks if you get the job for which you are interviewing. If you address all the following points when negotiating for this new position, you'll be well on your way to leadership success:

- **Negotiate to garner respect and equal status.** Your male peers are two to nine times more likely than you are to negotiate salary and other conditions such as administrative help, executive staff, bonus-earning parameters, and freedom to hire and fire prior to accepting an offer.[1] In their article "Women and Negotiations: Unveiling Some Secrets to Success," Martha W. Tack of Eastern Michigan University and Mindy S. McNutt of Wright State University say it more bluntly: "Failure to negotiate makes women appear weak, ignorant, and clueless albeit grateful and well-behaved in the workplace."[2] This is not how you want to be perceived when you start a new leadership position.

- **Ask for more money.** Right here, right now, I give you permission to do so. Initial salary offers are never the maximum available. The person doing the hiring might make it seem that way by challenging your credentials or experience. One of many women's biggest concerns is getting off on the wrong foot with a new boss. But consider this: How much money is it worth sacrificing to do this? If you obtained $11,000 more by negotiating for it during the interview for your first job, and then invested that plus the raises you subsequently received based on a percentage of your expanding salary, that money well invested would compound to over $1.5 million upon retirement.[3] Is it worth that much to you to be "liked" by anybody? Arm yourself with knowledge of what's fair and reasonable to request; for example, how much do comparable jobs pay? Don't limit yourself merely to an incremental increase over your current salary if your skills are in demand. Wait for your boss to make the first salary offer to ensure that you don't undervalue yourself.

- **Know what you want, and demonstrate how getting what you want will benefit the company.** Salary is only the beginning. What else will help the company retain you long term and avoid attrition costs? Flexible hours? Where you work? Pension contributions? Stock options? Vacation? Training? Women experience backlash when they demand such things; so don't *demand.*

  In the next section, we'll discuss better ways to acquire all of these things in a way that will also start your new work relationships off on a positive note. Other fringe benefits women don't often think about or ask for are:

  - Early performance reviews (for earlier raises)
  - Clarification in writing of the points on which your performance will be evaluated
  - Moving expenses (or a sign-on bonus that would cover them)
  - Health insurance
  - Exceptional performance bonuses
  - Prenegotiated support packages in the event of layoff

  But how does giving you all these goodies benefit the company? Health insurance locks you and your family into the corporate community; early reviews and bonuses encourage you to do your best; moving expenses can be a deal breaker.

- **Ask to meet all the key players with whom you'll be working once a serious offer is on the table.** You need to assess how many allies—and, especially, how many detractors—you'll have. Did someone in-house want this position? Who might sabotage you? Negotiate for the ability to fire any obstructers. Barring that, make certain before you accept the job that upper management will introduce you, explain to the entire staff why you got the job, and back you up as needed. *This is critical.* Otherwise, you risk open defiance and erosion of your status and power. Going to upper management for help after you're on board will position you as a weak leader who does not foresee problems and take action to nip them in the bud.

- **Negotiate up front to get the resources you need to get the job done.** Go for large victories but also as many small, frequent ones as you can accumulate. This is a rare, and crucial, window of opportunity to request needed resources. Such an opportunity may not come again easily—or at all. Does your group currently work with outdated software or hardware? Have too few people been doing too much for too long? Win the loyalty of your new team by lining up needed resources *before* you accept the position. Negotiate for people, tools, and a big enough budget to ensure your success from the get-go. You'll be asked to economize enough going forward. Recognizing and using this window of opportunity is one way to prove you have the "right stuff" as a leader.

- **Negotiate a powerful title.** This part of the negotiation alone can be very revealing about the organization's internal cultural attitudes toward women. To whom will you report? Who else reports to that person and what are their titles? Is yours comparable? If not, why not? Does the explanation seem legitimate, or vague? Have you done your homework to find out what the appropriate title should be, and how it should be compensated? The title may be a firm given, but don't treat it as an afterthought to be dismissed at the end of the negotiation. It can be your undoing if it leaves you open to others usurping your power, plum assignments, or territory. In tandem with negotiating your title, negotiate crystal-clear reporting relationships, and even where you and your staff will work. Don't allow yourself to be sequestered too far away from the seat of power.

- **Negotiate a career path.** State your ultimate objective and outline the most direct path. Get in writing what is expected at each stage so you can prepare to move up. This can be career-saving if supervisors leave the company, taking their promises to you with them.

- **Don't assume you have the power to hire, fire, compensate, or incentivize your staff.** This is especially true in union shops and family-owned firms. Get your specific powers in writing. This wins loyalty and legitimacy for you as a boss.

- **Don't fall into the frugality trap.** Women frequently think they can make an impression as leaders if they show they can do more with fewer resources, so they may not even ask for any. But working eighteen-hour days because you're short-handed, or can't afford more productive equipment, will not position you as a strong, savvy leader. It makes you look like you haven't graduated from the mid-level ranks.

How to Negotiate for Leadership Success

I've pointed out what you'll need to negotiate for success as you move up the ladder. Now let's look at how to do that successfully, so you will avoid the most common pitfalls.

The first big challenge women face is the prenegotiation anxiety that hits at 2 a.m. the night before the "big" interview. Scenarios race through our heads. What if we ask for what we want and then are criticized, challenged, rejected, and even demeaned? Our whole selves rebel against this process, which flies in the face of all our early training to please others and be liked. The road to victory seems very unclear, if not impossible to traverse. There don't seem to be any rules that work quite right for us.

But it's not about demanding or fighting for what we deserve. These actions merely prompt resistance and backlash. Instead, women's road to victory is paved with collaboration. Discuss what you want, what they need from you, what problems each of you face; then, when all this is out on the table, you can begin to negotiate a win-win solution. You have something to offer that they want, or they wouldn't be wasting this much time talking to you. Remember that at 2 a.m.

Before the big interview, do some homework about what the position is worth in the marketplace and what perks are standard. Merely requesting a 10 percent raise over your current salary might leave many thousands of dollars on the table, dollars that could buy you a better house or car, fund your child's college education, or cover your parents' assisted-living bills. *Don't* just ask your female peers what they're making—if they're underpaid, you'll trap yourself. Use the Internet, relatives, chamber of commerce, professional associations, your personal network (especially the men)—get real marketplace intelligence that you can point to statistically during the interview as backup for a big payday.

Being forearmed will help you avoid the common trap women face of undervaluing ourselves and therefore having low feelings of entitlement to higher levels of compensation. This is the inheritance of our gender's cultural training, and will doubtless hang around for several more generations—until there are enough role models to show us a better way. The sooner you realize that these feelings are your cultural legacy and don't reflect on you as an individual, the easier it will be to break the mold.

The only way to negotiate is from strength. Even if you will starve in the streets if you don't get this job, you've got to find the strength to be able to walk away from any exploitative situation. You say you feel too desperate right now to pull that off? Use that alter ego you created in Chapter 3.

Ideally, you already have a job and are negotiating for a better one. If so, be sure all your hard-won agreements are in writing and signed off on *before* you quit your current position. If the new employer refuses to do that, walk away.

The big interview is going well. You like them. They like you. When do you start negotiating seriously? Should you be the one to take the bull by the horns so they know where you're coming from?

No. Don't discuss salary, perks, title, power, or resources *until* they've offered you the position; let them make the first offer. At this moment, there are two traps you can fall into that will harm your credibility as a leader:

1. **The gratitude trap.** Women are usually so grateful for a job offer (and the "They like me! They really like me!" feeling that comes with it) that they accept it on the spot with whatever salary and perks are first offered. But this is the lowball offer and the starting point for negotiation. Even if this offer pays well above your old salary, comes with fantastic perks, and you are thrilled by your sudden windfall, hang back and counter with the highest number and best perk package you can factually substantiate. Engage in a dialogue about how you'll help them, why you're worth more than they're offering—experience, credentials, honors and awards, publications, record-breaking profits last quarter. Then take 48

hours before accepting, but don't say you have to talk it over with your spouse. You're the decision-maker; you're the leader.

2. **The "we can discuss it later" trap.** If negotiation is a stressful energy drain for you, you'll be tempted to sign the employment contract and "mop up the details afterwards." If you do, you'll have given away all your power to get what you want. Why should they say yes to anything further, if they've already signed you on and been rewarded for how cheaply you came on board?

What Organizations Can Do to Help Women Leaders Succeed

The focus of this chapter up to now has been on self-sufficiency. It has rested squarely on the shoulders of us as individual women to pull ourselves up by the bootstraps and improve our own negotiation skills. There is no thought of handouts; we don't want special help or favoritism. We want to be successful on our own merits.

That said, it behooves corporations to remove the impediments to female success that we are not in a position to address ourselves.

Corporations are losing out on genuine talent and the most qualified employees to lead projects/departments/divisions because women have been discouraged from asking for plum assignments and promotions. Aside from sometimes unpleasant competition from our male peers, we also discourage ourselves. We are trained to believe that hard work will garner these rewards and recognition, that choice assignments will be given to those who do the best work. We may have experienced backlash when asking in the past, so we sit back and wait for recognition and opportunities that never come. Meanwhile, we become dispirited when we see less talented and less committed employees, usually men, getting enviable raises and promotions. This leads directly to feeling underappreciated and resentful and may, subsequently, make you decide to leave the firm. A company needs to ask itself if business as usual is actually resulting in assigning the best person, not just the most vocal or aggressive person, to the job.

A corporate culture change, a simple one, could make all the difference in retaining and getting value from talented female employees. Instead of assigning projects and promotions to those who ask for them, managers should be directed to review the work of all employees at that level, male and female, and inquire across the board about their interests. Creating such a level playing field holds great potential for increasing productivity and diminishing attrition. Women who get stuck at mid-level jobs and watch less-qualified people promoted over them get discouraged and feel the need to jump to other firms in order to gain recognition.

Companies need to realize that, as leaders, women may be tested in ways to which men are never subjected. There will be questions about whether they got their job simply because a token female was needed, whether they're strong enough to make difficult decisions, whether their career path contains as much relevant experience as their male peers', and even whether they "slept their way to the top." All of these will be used by competitive employees who want the female leader's position, or who resent reporting to her. Upper management needs to keep these hazards in mind should negative reports about a female executive start filtering in. It is wise to consider the source and that person's agenda, even if the source is a trusted, long-time associate. There can be backlash when a woman moves outside of male colleagues' comfort zones, and it often takes the form of tarnishing her image, status, or reputation.

Companies will benefit from making an effort to seek out and recognize the employees, both male and female, who are working diligently and effectively (but quietly) behind the scenes. These are the people who need to be informed about opportunities for recognition and advancement. To formalize such an effort, mentoring programs facilitate recognition of the actual talent available within the company.

Companies that include gender as part of their diversity programs are going to be far ahead of the game in attracting the best talent. Smaller companies that don't or won't commit resources to diversifying their workforces will find themselves at a disadvantage. These firms will ultimately find themselves locked into one-dimensional ways of thinking, communicating, and marketing that are fast becoming outmoded. Such lack of depth and understanding of the modern marketplace (where women are often the decision-making consumers) will be detrimental to establishing relationships with larger and more desirable clients.

It is also expensive to lose executives. Screening and hiring costs, opportunity costs for employees conducting the hiring, and diminished productivity can cost a firm 150 percent of that lost executive-level worker's annual salary.[4] Keeping women challenged and appropriately rewarded boosts profits.

Although significant inroads have been made by women in the workforce who aspire to leadership roles, there still remains a lot to do. We need to recognize in ourselves what we bring to the table, and communicate that to our employers. The glass ceiling is cracking, but not yet completely down. We are currently representing a greater percentage of the workforce, and earning more college-level degrees than ever. Our future as leaders is bright, and there is no place to go but up. Use the information in this chapter and elsewhere to prevent mid-level stalling of your career path, and plan to mentor those behind you.

Discover Your Negotiation Skills:
The Path to Leadership—a New Position

The following fill-in-the-blank statements illustrate the critical points that must be hit when you are negotiating for a new position. An answer key is provided, but there are many ways you can phrase your answers, as long as they mean the same thing as the suggested responses.

1. Negotiate to _____ _____ and equal status.
2. Ask for more _____.
3. Know what you want, and _____ how getting what you want will benefit the company.
4. Ask to meet all the _____ _____.
5. Negotiate up front to get the _____ you need to get the job done.
6. Negotiate a powerful _____.
7. Negotiate a _____ path.
8. Don't assume you have the power to _____, _____, _____, or incentivize your staff.
9. Don't fall into the _____ trap.

Answer Key

1. garner respect
2. money
3. demonstrate
4. key players
5. resources
6. title
7. career
8. hire, fire, compensate
9. frugality

16

The Real Test:
Your Salary Negotiation

This chapter is intended to be a quick reference to the applicable tools discussed in previous chapters. However, I know some of you have turned straight to this page. You're negotiating a new job's salary (or a promotion or annual review) and you want to do it better than ever before. You don't have a lot of time; you don't want to memorize everything in this book or have the time right now to become a master negotiator: you really only want to succeed in the negotiation you're currently facing.

I understand. So, I've highlighted the key points for you to use right now and to give those whose aim is to become a master negotiator a quick refresher.

Before you begin any salary negotiation:

- Identify all parties' interests.
- Think of a collaborative solution that satisfies *your* needs.
- Determine how you will make the other party aware that you understand their needs and want to meet them.
- Decide how you will describe how the other party will get what they want while *you* get what *you* want.

Quick Tips: How to Maximize Your Salary

Chapter 1: Empower Yourself

- Change your mindset. You *do* deserve a lot of money for what you give the company, you don't have to threaten, and you will gain respect, not humiliation, by standing up for yourself.
- Go in intending to collaborate but do not back down on important issues.
- Research what those in comparable positions in your area are making. Show surprise if that's not what you are offered.
- If you have to concede on salary, get rewarded for it. Always. If they can't give you money, can they give you extra personal days? Vacation? Education? A car? A better work space? *Plan ahead for what you'll request* in exchange for any "no." Expect to be rewarded—both for good work and for all concessions you make.

Chapter 2: Your Style: Changes You Need to Make
When Negotiating with Men or Women

If you're negotiating with a male boss, emphasize your competence, knowledge, and the past year's accomplishments. If you're negotiating with a woman, demonstrate your enthusiasm for the job, your eagerness to take on more responsibility in the year ahead, and your commitment—she needs to trust you.

- Use inclusive language—"we" and "us."
- Emphasize your warmth and appreciation of others (but don't gush).
- Don't ask for more money for yourself—"I need a raise because I . . . ." Advocate for it on behalf of others—your family, your team, your clients—"A raise to this level will allow me to pay for longer day care for my children, and provide more time to our most important clients."
- Use external standards of fairness to protect yourself against being labeled "not nice"—"My research shows that people with my qualifications are receiving a minimum of 15 percent more than your

offer; if your pay is below industry standards, are there other available perks that might sweeten this offer?"

Chapter 3: How Not to Sabotage Your Negotiating Power

- Do your budget. How much does it cost to get to and from the job? Eat? Dress? Dry clean? Care for the kids? Make sure your new job's salary covers new expenses.
- Don't assume others know what you want, even if it's "obvious."
- Rationally analyze fears of being rejected, disliked, or humiliated.
- Experiment with an alter ego—walk in as a salary negotiation superstar (this chapter helps you create one).
- Turn your body into a power tool—straight posture, clear voice, and firm handshake radiate confidence, strength, and grace.

Chapter 4: The Four Stages of Negotiation

- Remember the four stages of negotiation:
    1. Planning and preparation
    2. Opening and setting the tone
    3. Idea and information exchange
    4. Closing strategies that ensure commitment and performance.
- The most important phase in a salary negotiation is planning and preparation:
    - List your accomplishments
    - Research what others (especially males) are being paid
    - Be familiar with industry standards
    - Know your company's financial situation
- Make a list of what you think your boss wants, and how you can provide it.
- Don't rush the stages.
- Take control of the opening: "I'm looking forward to a prosperous year for both of us." "I've enjoyed working with you this past year—I feel I've learned and grown a lot."
- In the idea stage, find out how you can make yourself more valuable going forward.

- Close with commitments on both sides—if you do X, they'll further compensate with Y.

Chapter 5: Determine Which Negotiation Style Is Right for You
- Go to Chapter 5 right now and determine your negotiation style. This will take only five minutes, and it's a real eye-opener.

Chapter 6: Manage Negotiations with the "Backwards Mapping" Technique
- Plan backwards to achieve a successful outcome if you have a specific salary/perks goal in mind that will require a more complex negotiation.
- Strategize the right issues and the right time to introduce them.
- Communicate your full value, and how to include the influence of allies.
- Develop a walk-away strategy if you don't reach agreement.

Chapter 7: Offensive Maneuvers and How to Counter Them
- Don't use hardball tactics even if your boss uses them; you'll face backlash if you do.
- Gain respect by masterfully deflecting them.
- If your boss tries to postpone your raise, ask questions about:
    1. Why this is important to the company
    2. When you might expect a raise
    3. What they might do for you meanwhile
- Recognize tactics such as postponing your raise meeting several times, "take it or leave it" offers, calling your competence into question, or a show of false anger. Be aware that these are often tactics and not indicative of your value, and can be effectively countered if you're prepared.
- Don't let your fears rule your actions.

Chapter 8: Power Moves for Handling Difficult People
- Know your boss. Is he or she intentionally difficult—a hardball player? Accidentally difficult—with good intentions but controlling rather than collaborative? Unfulfilled—someone whose needs are not met?

- Diagnose; don't react.
- Join your boss's team; change the game of you vs. your boss into us against the world.
- Make it easy and pleasurable for your boss to say yes to your desires.
- Use the planning worksheet for dealing with difficult people.

Chapter 9: Communication Strategies That Create a Level Playing Field

- Take on the adult responsibility of changing your early conditioning.
- Take control of the negotiation—gracefully and effectively.
- Describe your accomplishments with phrases that make it easy for your boss to agree.
- State your reasons for how you approach problems and offer competent solutions.
- Never use the word "but" in a salary negotiation; rephrase your sentence to start with "Yes, that's right . . ." or "Yes, that's possible . . . here are some barriers we need to brainstorm our way around."
- Ask your boss to clarify in detail any sweeping generalizations about your work so you know precisely how to improve.
- Above all, *don't* overwhelm your boss with a thousand reasons why you deserve a raise. The human brain is easily overloaded. Stick with your strongest three arguments and emphasize them several times.

Chapter 10: Fail-Proof Persuasion Tactics

- Determine which of the six primary persuasion tactics might best persuade your boss:
    1. Hero strategy: Make the boss feel important
    2. Rational persuasion: Use facts and figures
    3. Inspirational appeal: Motivate through appeal to values or aspirations
    4. Morality appeal: Encourage the boss to do the right thing
    5. Coalition tactic: Get more influential others to plead your case
    6. Reciprocal tactic: "You scratch my back; I'll scratch yours"

Chapter 11: The Art of the Redirect: Managing Destabilizing Moves

- When confronted by diminishing or demeaning moves, use a redirect that deflects the challenge without making you look harsh, angry, or out of control:
  1. Insert time: Pause to reflect.
  2. Insert space: Take a bathroom break.
  3. Verbally label what the person is doing and calmly call the person on it.
  4. Quietly question assumptions.
  5. Factually correct errors or misstatements.
  6. Divert focus away from a personal attack onto the bigger professional issue at hand.

Chapter 12: Gender Intelligence and Negotiation

- If you are negotiating with a male boss, schedule your meeting for between 3 and 5 p.m. (assuming he's not jet-lagged), when the male brain is chemically less aggressive and more collaborative.

Chapter 13: How, When, and Why to Make Concessions

- If you must make concessions to your boss about money or perks, make sure every concession is rewarded with either tangible compensation or intangible rewards.
- *Do not* concede to yourself before you ever get to the table. Make your boss say no to you; don't say no to yourself!
- Make your boss work hard and wait for every concession. Conceding quickly to please the other person works well in our personal lives but encourages disrespect in a business setting.
- *Do not* fill the gap with unrequested concessions if your boss meets your requests with silence. Silence is a powerful tactic; don't be a victim. Meet silence with silence.
- Plan your concessions in advance. If your boss doesn't give you exactly what you want, determine what an acceptable alternative would be.

Chapter 14: Negotiating with the "Big Boys"

- If you are negotiating compensation at a very high level, use the Negotiation Mapping Model, which includes:
  1. Backwards mapping to your objectives
  2. All party listing
  3. Counterpart values assessment
  4. Dealing with high-stakes emotions
  5. Barriers audit
  6. Creating a plan
  7. Delivering on the opportunity

Chapter 15: Negotiate Your Way to Leadership Success

- If you are undertaking a leadership role, critical points to hit in your compensation negotiation include:
  1. Negotiating title and salary level that will garner peer respect and equal status
  2. Demonstrating how perks like location, stock options, and flexible hours will benefit the company
  3. Making it a condition that you meet and speak with all key players before you sign an employment contract
- Be sure to negotiate:
  1. Needed resources up front, not after the offer is accepted
  2. A future career path and a (hopefully unnecessary) parting package
- Obtain the power to hire, fire, and incentivize staff—don't assume that it is a given, especially in family-owned businesses or union shops.
- Avoid these common traps:
  1. The frugality trap: Trying to gain points by doing more with fewer staff and resources or lower budget. Bringing in new resources (if needed, of course) creates respect and earns the loyalty of your new staff.
  2. The "we can discuss it later; we'll mop up the details once you're on board" trap: Get every promise in writing in your contract; otherwise you may be setting yourself up to fail.

3. The timeless trap: Be sure your contract specifies timelines for all promises.

It's time to make the gap between male and female salaries go away, and with the tools provided in this book, you stand poised to start making a difference. Use them for yourself first and then be a role model for your daughter, your niece, and all the young women behind you who will emulate your success.

Discover Your Personal Goals: Salary Negotiation

Answering the questions in the following two worksheets will prepare you for any salary negotiation:

PREPARATION WORKSHEET

1. Employment position: _____

2. What is the "market value"—the current salary range—for this position? _____ Sources for this information include:
   - Websites such as wetfeet.com, quintcareers.com, salary.com
   - Government salary surveys such as iseek.com, Find a job, Find Salary information
   - Trade and professional organizations' members' salary surveys and want ads
   - Your network of contacts for informational interviews
   - Employment agencies
   - Competitors

3. What is the employer's salary range? _____

4. What do I consider a satisfactory offer? _____

5. What will my opening request be? (should be 5 to 10 percent above expected figure) _____

6. What credentials, skills, and accomplishments justify my requested salary? State these in specific terms: examples of work
you've performed, past results in quantifiable terms, and so on.

_____

_____

7. What objections might the employer have to my request?

_____

_____

8. How will I respond to these objections?

_____

_____

9. What nonsalary items such as benefits, stock options, and perks
do I have to negotiate for or trade in exchange for salary?

_____

_____

10. What combination of salary and benefits is the minimum I will
accept?

_____

_____

NEGOTIATION WORKSHEET

1. Market value/competitive salary for this position is: $_____
2. My opening request will be: $_____
3. My bottom-line acceptable salary is: $_____
4. Nonsalary negotiable items include:

_____

_____

_____

_____

_____

Satisfactory salary/benefits package would be:

$_____ + _____

_____

_____

Prepare your opening statement in writing:

_____

_____

_____

_____

_____

Prepare your justification (use specific examples to support your request):

1. _____

_____

2. _____

_____

3. _____

_____

17

Put Your Negotiation Skills to Work

I am going to begin and end this chapter discussing personal values as they impact negotiation. You've seen (and I hope interacted with) the Discover Your Personal Values exercises I've included throughout this book. It's important that you use these skills for the good of yourself and others.

You can't know what your terms are until you know what
your personal values are.

Negotiation skills in and of themselves are neutral, like any tool. It's how they are used that makes the difference. You can negotiate for money, fame, and power; for education, cooperation, and relationship-building; or for circumstances that unintentionally ruin someone's life. You may do these things with deliberate focus or they may be by-products of your focus on other goals. I encourage you to consider both short- and long-term consequences when you go out into the world armed with these new abilities to influence, achieve, and acquire. Be careful what you wish—and then negotiate—for.

When I named the first chapter "Empower Yourself," my goal was that we women remove the cultural blinders we were raised to accept and that cause so many of the struggles we experience when we sit at today's negotiating tables.

I don't want you to be one of these women. I want this generation of women to amass all the money, power, and influence that their substantial talents deserve. I want enough senior executive women in place in corporations around the world so that every young woman who wants a mentor can have one with whom she can easily identify. As women undertake to introduce our particular style of negotiation, we will permanently influence America's (and the world's) corporate cultures.

It's time to stop thinking that being nice, thoughtful, humble, and appropriate are bargaining weaknesses. It's time to stop giving anger and meanness the undeserved respect they have acquired and to call them on the carpet for what they are—short-sighted and ineffective in today's business milieu. We have plenty of problems to tackle in this country, and they're not going to get better unless we start bringing our style of long-term relationship-building to America's bargaining tables.

One thing most professional and non-career-oriented women both know is that the male style of negotiation does not work for us. We hate it, even as under pressure we've mastered its nuances. It has garnered us neither the credibility that men require of negotiating partners ("She's being false; trying too hard") nor the trust that women require ("She's too hard-driving; that makes me uncomfortable"). Backlash has damaged far too many women's careers.

The greatest power we as females have is authenticity. If we apply it strategically (without sharing *every* thought or emotion), we can quickly get to the core of what the majority of negotiating partners want. Giving all sides what they want (and more!) is the art of negotiation, not one-upmanship and power plays.

If you started reading this book thinking you had very little power, I hope you've discovered that's not true and have revised your self-image accordingly. Even a few minor adjustments internally will create a ripple effect you may already have started to feel (if so, keep going!). I know such changes are not easy for anyone to make, and I applaud those of you who have. If you're hanging back, I encourage you to try just one or two of the tools I've offered. Prove to yourself their value.

At the very least, make sure you are not sabotaging yourself. It's one thing to have others hold you back, but holding yourself back just makes no sense. As mothers, wives, sisters, and friends we've been taught many behaviors that work in those roles but that don't translate well into our role as businesswomen. You don't have to change those behaviors in your personal life, but to succeed in your professional life, just start using some of the new tools I've provided in this book.

Have you ever had a dream where you were in a play, but you didn't know your lines, or hadn't rehearsed but were suddenly onstage on opening night? That's how it feels when women without prior training walk into negotiations. Many of us would sacrifice that half million dollars I mentioned earlier in this chapter to avoid such feelings. With a little knowledge, such as knowing the normal stages through which negotiations progress, you can feel like a star at the table. It's not difficult. These stages are easy to identify and work through with planning and forethought. I have done this myself, and I know the power that a little preparation gives you. Never sell yourself short—it can make all the difference to your ultimate career success. You *can* know, going in, how to handle the majority of deal disruptors.

You, Too, Can Be a Power Player

Has anyone ever sat you down to help you figure out what your negotiation style is? Probably not. Most women can give elaborate descriptions of their work passion or fashion style but draw a blank when asked about their negotiation style. This is critical, and once you've identified it, you will be able to maximize your strengths and work on your weaknesses. If you know your own hot buttons, you are far more able to prevent anyone from pushing them, especially in the heat of the bargaining. And knowing all potential negotiation styles allows you to counter the moves of others. That's what I call power.

Power players have known for a long time that the most important part of any negotiation happens behind the scenes. They know how to create allies, control agendas, stage ideal settings, and, most important, when to walk away and regroup. Women untrained in the art of negotiation may find these concepts shallow and manipulative; yet once you study such moves you'll recognize them because you've used them in everyday life. Who hasn't discussed an upcoming date with a friend, planned what to wear, brainstormed about a venue, and brought enough money for cab fare home, just in case? The art of the win-win collaboration is being very clear about what you want, and finding out as much as you can about what others want. From there, making it happen is all about getting the right people on board. You can do this!

That said, facing power players at the negotiating table can be intimidating—a bit like David going up against Goliath. If you're ever in this position, the defensive strategies provided in Chapter 7 against such attack moves should be the slingshots you need to confidently face them. Confidence is by far the biggest part of the negotiation game. If you walk in knowing you're equipped for just about everything they can throw at you, then you've already joined their ranks. Think like a power player, know that you are one, and act like it. That will take you far, if you do it all with grace and collaboration.

Remember that there is a lot of power in being able to set the scene and agenda of a negotiation. Grab all or any part of that power that you can. Other players often feel this is the function of an administrative assistant— clean the conference room and type up the agenda so the executives can do their thing. You know better. You'll know how to prepare, whom to get on board, and even the best seat to claim for power and status (if need be before anyone else arrives). You will know what homework you need to do and how to do it. You'll be ahead of the game, and that builds confidence.

However, all the confidence in the world will not prevent others from being difficult negotiators. For women, who've been trained to accommodate and treat others with kindness and compassion, this can turn into a situation where we are made uncomfortable or feel manipulated. We've been trained to stay open to the needs of others, not to take the reins and turn such challenges into opportunities. But there is nothing ungracious about finding out how a difficult person's needs can be melded with yours to create a win-win. That, in fact, is the height of graciousness and something to which we should all aspire. It takes strength to handle the negative emotions such people can create in us, but the tools in Chapter 8 will have given you methods to focus upon that will bring most opponents around to your way of thinking. Appreciation, connection, respect for others and their accomplishments are all ingrained behaviors in many of us; they also happen to be effective tools for breaking down resistance. Start with understanding your opponents' way of thinking first; then walk side by side while you guide them down *your* path. You'll get there.

If you want to make things happen, you have to act the part of someone who is capable of making them happen. Women are trained to be good listeners, and this is a very critical negotiating skill. However, if we make it our go-to stance, we give away power. Just deciding to respond to what the other party offers is too passive, and hands over control of the proceedings to others. It might seem like the "nice" thing to do, to be respectful and listen to their side, but you're not being "nice" to yourself if you let them set the tone and take their preferred direction throughout. State up front what *you* want to accomplish. Then start listening. This will position you in their minds as someone who is not a pushover, who needs to be respected and engaged.

Although there may be a thousand reasons why you should get what you want, don't try to list them. I can't emphasize this enough. The human mind can handle only so much information; therefore, bring to the table your two or three biggest arguments, and repeat them if necessary. Don't bring up the next and the next and the next. Your counterparts will tune out and ignore you; you will have shut them down mentally. Stick to your biggest guns.

Use the word "no" as little as possible. It, too, creates mental shutdowns. Whenever possible, substitute the phrase, "Yes, and . . . ." This takes some getting used to, but you'll rapidly see the difference in how others respond.

You, Too, Can Handle Challenges like a Pro

In the end, it's all about persuading the other party to recognize and fulfill your interests. Make them feel like heroes, be ready with all the salient facts, inspire them, appeal to their moral code, confront them with your team, or simply scratch their backs. Women have an intuitive edge when it comes to sensing which persuasion tactics are likely to work best in any given situation. Those tactics were withheld from many of us as youngsters, and we've had to make a lot of mistakes in order to discover them for ourselves.

But maybe I'm making it sound too easy. I've been on the front lines; I know it isn't. There truly are numerous things that cause women genuine concern before entering a negotiation. Being challenged for what we don't know or who we are; being demeaned and called ridiculous; having our heartfelt, emotional responses critiqued and used against us to damage our credibility; and even being threatened. All these sap our power if we don't know effective countermoves. And how in the world can we also stay in touch with graciousness at the same time? It's a lot to ask.

But again, you can train yourself to handle such challenges, and you already have the tools: for example, giving yourself time and space, calling a move what it is instead of responding blindly, questioning instead of being defensive or angry, even correcting the other's perception so it nips confrontations in the bud. What does it take to control an angry response? How do you throw a challenge calmly back into another person's lap? You've likely done this with family members, and it's vital that you do it at the negotiation table, too. When the other side sees that you are able to maintain your cool under pressure, such challenges will subside; no one tries negotiation tactics more than once if they don't work. Then it's in your power to steer things toward a more collaborative tone.

The good news is, the days of women training themselves to act more like men are beginning to be seen for what they truly were—ineffective and nonproductive. That's like trying to ask a lioness to act more like a horse; she can, a little, but it leaves all her best stuff behind.

Industrial and technological societies of the last two centuries have hobbled themselves by relying too heavily on the strengths of only one gender. Challenging a woman's credibility because she operates on a different level used to be effective at keeping women down; now, at an ever-increasing number of companies, it just looks ignorant.

The real strength that women bring to the bargaining table is authenticity and grace. Grace is not possible without authenticity; grace cannot be faked. And in the world of negotiation, nowhere is grace more powerful than when we must make concessions. It is not possible to negotiate without making concessions unless you hold all the cards, and even then, if you force your opponent to knuckle under just because you can, you've still failed. No one likes to be forced into powerless failure; in long-term relationships, such as today's business world increasingly demands, the resentment this breeds will come back to hurt, or cost, you.

In reality, making concessions is a given, and therefore needs to be done strategically and for one's own maximum power and benefit. A danger women face is that we often concede our power before it's ever tested. I hope that this book has, at the very least, taught you that you no longer need to do this. Get rewarded for every concession you make! Every single one! In your personal *and* your professional life! Men expect it; now, so should you.

And be gracious when others concede to you. It may be thrilling, it may be invigorating, and it's most certainly validating when the other side concedes, but it's a rookie mistake to gloat. Always strive to keep on an equal and dignified level with your opponents if you want to do business with them again down the road. Accept their concessions gracefully, and reward them as you expect them to reward you. At the very least, a simple "thank you" in acknowledgment of their concession never hurts.

I also think it is grace that gets a woman up into the big leagues. A woman who is able to make people feel good about $100,000 deals is more likely to be offered $1 million and $1 billion opportunities. A woman who can successfully network, and create a string of successes on her way up, creates a portfolio that opens such doors.

But as with the game of chess, as you master your fundamental moves, the game becomes more complex. Eventually, you find yourself playing a 3-D chess game, and in business, you eventually engage in 3-D negotiations. Here is where you think in big, long-term, and world-changing terms. It is here that you must involve larger numbers of powerful players, institutions, and governments. And yet, it will still come down to what I've referred to again and again—collaboration and win-win. At this level, there are players powerful enough to impose their wills and extract punishing concessions; and it will be at this level that women can help mitigate some of the more damaging fallout these moves can cause long term. This is where our ability to come up with creative, collaborative solutions is desperately needed. It has been "big boys" for a long stretch; now it's time for the "big girls." We're beginning to march in, armed and ready for the challenges.

As you master negotiation skills, attaining greater positions of responsibility is inevitable. You'll be able to make things happen, meet sales targets, manage staff, create and cultivate important client relationships—you will simply become a greater and more valuable commodity in the marketplace. This is when the opportunity to lead will present itself, and you will have to make a decision about your life direction.

Leadership is not for everyone, but for those with solid negotiation skills, it is a natural fit. Leadership is all about negotiating with people to get things done the way you and your company want them done. It's also about creating your own opportunities to succeed: setting up new positions so that success is almost inevitable and even your exit is well compensated and contributes to continued upward mobility. It's about marshalling resources and rallying troops, positioning yourself so that others are not forced, but inspired, to follow you.

Women have seen men fight for and demand what they feel they deserve. We've seen our fathers and husbands come home looking beat up, whether failed or successful, after giving it their best shot. We've recoiled from the idea of going in and pounding our fists on our boss's desk as we insist on a raise or a promotion. And even if we've had the courage to go in and do this, we've rarely gotten what we wanted; most likely we've been punished and stalemated at a permanent mid-level in our careers just for daring to do so.

The business media has been full of stories about women quitting corporate America in droves, seemingly to "devote more time to family," but really out of lack of fulfillment of our true ambitions to succeed and lead. There has been a gut-level feeling that there must be another way, but there are too few role models to show us what it is. I am pleased to be able to introduce you to a few of those still-too-rare role models in the next chapter, and I trust you will find them as inspiring as I do.

The most successful way for women to negotiate (which I've proven to myself and the women who've gone through my Leadership Institute) is to focus on collaboration. Collaboration works for women. It motivates others to unblock opportunities we seek and prevents the backlash that stalls out careers. Instead of making our meeting with our bosses about what *we* want, we make it about what *they* want. And then we give it to them, in return for clearly negotiated compensation. In turn, they give us more opportunities to duplicate our successes, and we make more money. They win, and we win—on our terms.

The Importance of Values to Negotiations and Leadership

As I mentioned when we first started this chapter, I want to begin and end with a discussion about values. There are three important lessons about values and their impact on negotiations that I hope you'll take away from this book:

1. Your values are, and should be, unique to you. Never accept another person's values as your own without questioning, examining, and testing them in your own life. Even your parents' values, the ones you grew up with and believe as gospel truth, should at some time in your adult life be objectively judged. Otherwise, you'll be unconsciously ruled by the opinions of others, which may not serve your deepest and most authentic interests fully or adequately.

2. You may not know what your real values are until they are tested under pressure.

3. Dealing with situations where your values conflict reveals which values are most important to you, and which will be either discarded or reworked. Shades of gray may temporarily obscure your vision and rock your self-identity, but you will ultimately learn the truth of what's most important to you by observing the consequences of your own actions.

Values translated into working practices are templates for behavior that clarify how you will lead in your work environment. Let's take the word "integrity" as an example of a definition of a value translated into a leadership principle:

As a value: Integrity means telling the whole truth to others and operating within the law in all business concerns.

As a leadership principle: Integrity means that in order to create a workplace environment that supports telling the whole truth one-on-one and in meetings, I will model that behavior myself.

The missing step in most values exercises is making your values actionable. Chances are you have participated in at least one program or group session defining your values and those of your organization. In too many cases, these lists of values remain on the flip chart or in your notebook, because there is no focus on practicing your values. Putting those values into practice is crucial for authentic leaders because, under pressure—in the loneliness of leadership—the only values you can count on are those that you have already tested and proved during your life.

Your leadership principles are an outgrowth of your values; they are the linchpin that links your values to the true compass of your leadership.

These final values exercises are ones that I think you will use frequently throughout your life. It brings into focus all the other values exercises and provides a good compass when trying to decide the best direction to take.

Discover Your Personal Values: Testing Your Ethical Boundaries

To begin, imagine that you are facing a challenge in your work or home life. You are about to take actions that will become the headline on the front page of the newspaper that you and everyone you know reads every day. Would you be proud or ashamed to have your colleagues, family, and friends read about your actions in stark, big, black and white letters?

1. Close your eyes and listen to your intuition.
2. Imagine telling your partner, your parents, or your child about your decision and your actions.

3. Take a deep breath and get in touch with the sensations of your body and its surroundings.

4. Ask yourself: What is the "right" thing for me to do in this situation? What would I want that headline to say?

_____

_____

_____

_____

If your answer is that you would not be proud to have that headline published, perhaps you should reexamine your behavior, and look for ways to modify it. A far more creative and satisfying solution may be just around the corner.

Discover Your Personal Values: Identifying Your Leadership Principles

Do the values exercise below to help you get in touch with the principles you bring to your role as a leader.

The purpose of this exercise is to translate your values into leadership principles. Take each value and definition you have previously created in the various exercises in this book and turn them into concrete and visible leadership principles. What action will you take to support that value?

Use the action table below to record the leadership principles you will use in leading others. Once you have translated these values into leadership principles, rate yourself on how well you currently are putting those principles into practice. Use a 1 to 5 scale (1 = I'm failing to put this principle into practice; 3 = I'm doing an average job; 5 = I'm doing an excellent job of putting this principle into practice).

VALUE NAME	LEADERSHIP PRINCIPLE	RATING
_____	_____	_____
_____	_____	_____
_____	_____	_____

_____   _____   _____
_____   _____   _____
_____   _____   _____

What has been hard about putting those principles into practice?

_____
_____
_____

What steps can I take tomorrow to put my leadership principles into practice?

_____
_____
_____

18

View from the Trenches:
Lessons for Women as Leaders
and Negotiators

As more executive women chip through the glass ceiling, they earn experience and have stories to tell that offer lessons to future generations of executive women. Their value as mentors to younger aspiring executives, both male and female, is impossible to calculate. And alongside them, in the corridors and adjacent offices, are men who make choices either to help or to hinder their progress.

This chapter contains interviews with two women who made it to the upper echelons of corporate America in part by deploying superior negotiating skills, along with many other attributes that made them successful. We discuss the challenges they faced on their journey toward the C-suite, as well as the advice they would give to those following the trails they have blazed. We also talk to men who support the advancement of women in their own workplaces.

Women as Leaders and Negotiators:
The Female Perspective

Betty Rengifo Uribe, EdD, Executive Vice President, California Bank & Trust

Yasmin: What was your journey to get where you are today like?

Dr. Betty: My journey has been full of ups and downs, with the downs full of lessons learned. I grew up in Colombia, South America. I was twelve years old when my mother sat my three brothers and me down for a serious conversation. She was tired of the life she was living with my father and wanted to leave the country. My father, a self-made millionaire, suffered from alcoholism, and my mother was subjected to spousal abuse and my father's infidelity. I was daddy's little girl so the decision to come to the U.S. was not an easy one. Upon arrival in the U.S., we became instantly poor. We lived with my aunt Ruby who taught me etiquette and the basics of the English language, and told me: "One day you will be dining with the president of the United States. No one in this world is better than you—even the president gets up in the morning, brushes his teeth, and puts on his clothes just like you do." Little did she know that I would be dining with President Bush Sr. less than fifteen years later. My mother taught me early on to live with a higher purpose. She would say: "Make a difference for others, don't just go in pursuit of money; the money will come when you do what you're passionate about." I remember having visitors at our little apartment, when my mother would say: "You get to share your clothes and your bed because they have even less than we do and God has blessed us with a roof over our head." She was always so grateful; we never knew we were poor. I began to clean houses to help with the household expenses, and practically raised my little brother, who was six years old at the time.

Very early in my life my mother told me: "Mijita, you are super intelligent; you can do anything you put your heart in, you just need to work hard and study hard." I believed that, and growing up I worked harder than those around me and studied hard to get good grades, making myself better all the time. Many times during my career and in my personal life I have faced circumstances that seemed bigger than life at the time. I always remember these lessons, realizing that my only obstacle is in my own head.

Yasmin: Betty, tell me about your career trajectory.

Dr. Betty: I started my first business at the age of nineteen; it was an engineering and manufacturing company where we manufactured surgical lighting components. I have since owned several businesses in the U.S., and in South America when my father passed away. I started my banking career in 1988 as a personal banker, and quickly moved up the career ladder, becoming the youngest branch manager one and a half years later, where I was tagged "The Quicker Picker-Upper." I took branches, regions, and organizations that were broken or underperforming and quickly became the person who was called upon to turn them around. Education has been a big part of my journey; I firmly believe that education is one of the biggest differentiators. My doctorate has opened up doors for me and my organization; personally it has given me the opportunity to see things through a different lens and a higher purpose. I've had mentors along the way from the very beginning. My first mentor was the CEO of a bank in Orange County. He taught me how to see the bank (and life) from a strategic perspective, and how all the pieces of the puzzle fit together. I remember him saying to me: "When I'm on my death bed, it won't matter how much money I made, the titles I collected, or the places I've been; what will matter most is the people I have touched along the way." Today I have mentors in every area of my life: spirituality, family, relationship, health, career, education, community, and recreation.

Studies show that there are two areas where we have the biggest growth in our climb up the leadership ladder. One is when we begin to manage managers; the other is when we get to report directly to the CEO managing a line of business. I've had a big learning curve reporting to the CEO for the past three years as I've learned to work with other executives, daily perfecting the art of effective negotiation. It's a journey.

The idea of enrollment is very important. When you are selling something to someone, it's about you. When you are asking someone to do something—enrolling them—it's about them. Ask them what their vision is and make sure your vision is aligned with theirs. Look for *their* higher purpose; then it comes from them. By doing that, I've gotten myself invited into the White House, the Pentagon, and the presidential palace in Colombia, my native country. I've been named a designee (someone who represents Colombian interests in the United States) for the Colombian-American Chamber in Washington, D.C., and met personally with the president of Colombia.

Yasmin: How do you define negotiating?

Dr. Betty: Negotiation happens when two or more people make a decision that will affect everyone present. It's the ability to get everyone to walk away feeling that the end result of the decision was fair. Before I step into the negotiating table, I decide the minimum I'm willing to walk away with, and it becomes easy after that. The idea is to step into the negotiating table with a willingness to create a win-win.

Yasmin: Do you have to get all your votes lined up before you get to the table?

Dr. Betty: I normally work with people individually before I get to the table. Big decisions are made outside of the table, one person at a time. When everyone comes together, there is a common agreement already as the heavy lifting has already been done.

Yasmin: Women don't even know how to do that. My thing is to teach them how. You can't take the risk of losing at the table. How do you enroll people when negotiating?

Dr. Betty: I always look for people's intrinsic motivation. To be a great leader you have to take the time to get to know people around you, meaning not just your employees but your peer group and your boss, your community, and the people around you, at a personal level. People don't care how much you know until they know how much you care. It's really your actions that show that you care. Some of my people used to say, "I'm not good at sales." I replied, "I don't want you to sell; I want you to create trusting relationships for generations." When people trust you, your job becomes easier all around.

Yasmin: A lot of women think it's manipulative when other women are strategic about their personal leadership brand. Do women know you are very strategic?

Dr. Betty: Yes, I make it very public.

Yasmin: How do they respond?

Dr. Betty: I tell my people and mentees it is important to pay close attention to their leadership brand. What we do is a mirror of who we are. There is a saying: "Your actions are so loud, I can't hear what you're saying." It is our actions that people use to determine if they can trust us with their careers, their families, and their future. When I tell people I am strategic about my leadership brand, they are both surprised and inspired. I let people know how and why I operate strategically and create trust very quickly. It's really easy to build trust when I am transparent—what you see is what you get.

Yasmin: How do you handle presenting, or downplaying, your femininity during negotiations?

Dr. Betty: My femininity is part of what I bring to the table. My composite female left-right brain reasoning complements the male cognitive reasoning. One of the things that men do very, very well, and I have learned to do, is create relationships away from the table. I'll say, "Hey, I'm going to be bringing this up at the meeting. I need your support." So, by the time I get to the table, I already have champions, people who are ready to say, "Absolutely yes, I agree with Betty."

A "no," to me, is a "not yet."

Yasmin: And you know that's how men think about "no"—it means "not yet." You can take that good male energy and work with it.

Dr. Betty: Many women I know take "no" personally. I've seen men argue during a negotiation and then go out and have a good game of golf afterward. It's not personal, it's just business.

Yasmin: Men are used to rejection; they have to go after women. For women, "no" means rejecting who we are at the core.

Dr. Betty: But it's not at all personal. A "no" means the way that I positioned it is not aligned with what's important to them at the time. I look at it objectively, rather than feeling I'm being attacked—this is hugely important.

You have to be comfortable in your own skin in order to be detached. These messages women tell themselves—"I'm not enough; I have to be right; I have to look good"—they're what I call "your little committee." When somebody touches those triggers, then your committee begins to say, "I told you, you weren't good enough!" In order to get rid of that committee, you've got to be able to understand you are good, bad, and ugly, and be OK with it.

Guys don't think, "What do I look like?" "Are they going to like me?" No, they think, "Let's get to the point, negotiate, and get it done." That's where women fail in negotiation, because we are completely attached—take rejection personally—instead of maintaining who we are and staying on task.

Yasmin: Describe your leadership style and how it affects your approach to negotiation.

Dr. Betty: I am collaborative by nature; I make decisions by consensus and I am also aware that I have the veto power when the team doesn't align. I am extremely self-aware. So I try to be completely vulnerable, completely truthful. In negotiation, that vulnerability puts me (and women) in a position of power. It's completely disarming, because everybody has things that might embarrass them.

Yasmin: How do you enroll men in your vision?

Dr. Betty: I find that a lot of the men have a higher purpose having to do with society, their family, their impact, their epitaph when they die, their legacy. This is especially true of men in their late forties or fifties. I am aware of that. I usually find commonalities between their vision and my vision, and focus on that common area when I talk about my vision. I make sure my vision augments or adds to their vision in order to create a win-win.

Yasmin: What areas do you think are the most difficult for women to overcome in negotiating conditions for leadership success?

Dr. Betty: One of the most difficult areas for women to overcome in negotiation is right between their ears. The lies we tell ourselves, especially if we are negotiating with someone of power. We must realize that we are just as good as anyone else and have the confidence to step into the negotiating table. Do our homework and be ready to create win-wins.

Yasmin: What would you advise women who want a career trajectory leading to executive leadership?

Dr. Betty: In addition to having mentors, have champions along the way; someone who will endorse you and take the time to champion you and your cause. Give it away. Don't ever forget where you came from; reach back and take others with you. Be confident in your ability to do the job; if you are in your position it's because you're good enough. Don't compete against others, compete against the best version of yourself and always strive to grow. Be humble and genuinely care about the people around you and have a higher purpose for what you do. Be authentic and vulnerable. It's counterintuitive to think that power and vulnerability can cohabit; most people think in order to have power, you can't be vulnerable. What I've experienced is: The more vulnerable you are, the more powerful you are able to be. Be a continuous learner. Make yourself better each day so you always have a better you to give to others. And finally, take care of you. Have balance in your life. When you take care of you, you create the ability to take care of others. Your actions are the example of who you really are.

Graciela Meibar, former Vice President Global Diversity, Mattel, Inc.

Yasmin: Graciela, growing up, were you the kind of kid that just went for it?

Graciela: I've always been a risk taker. My parents were poor; sending me to college was a huge drain, and I was the first in the family to be able to go to college. Most of my girlfriends only finished high school. I wanted to get a college degree.

I got my BA from USC and an MBA at Pepperdine. To me that was validation, the removal of a roadblock. I sacrificed. I remember my father saying to me, "You don't have a life. You're studying all the time." I said, "My time will come."

The year 2003 was difficult. My job was changing. Mattel wanted me to go to Miami with the entire Latin American division. My father was very ill here in L.A. My marriage was in the bricks. Moving to Miami was not an option for me.

I said to Mattel, "I'm not moving even if it means leaving the company." I was frightened, absolutely, but I was honest. The head of Human Resources came to me and said, "We don't want to lose you. We would love for you to become our diversity leader. We know that we need to improve the sales skills of the organization. Because of your background, we think you can do that." I immediately said, "Why diversity? Why me? Because I'm the Latina in the mix?" But they said, "No, because you know Mattel so well." I liked that answer.

Yasmin: Describe your leadership style and how it affects your approach to negotiation.

Graciela: Mattel's CEO told me, "Whenever you come into my office and you have an agenda, I know that eventually I'm going to give you what you want." It's because I come with passion, but my passion is well founded.

Yasmin: How are you able to balance your passion and warmth and yet draw the line so people don't mess with you?

Graciela: One thing I believe most women have is intuition. We can sense a rat a mile away. When people lie to me or fudge the truth, I feel it. You have to set your boundaries early on.

For example, my door is always open, but I immediately sense when the person coming through has a hidden agenda. Maybe it's the words they use, their body language. If somebody is talking to me and looking over there, maybe they're shy, but when I begin to feel that there's something amiss, I call it as it is: "This is what I heard. What's going on here?" I ask for verification. I have developed the ability to be analytical.

Yasmin: Self-confidence is important when it comes to trusting your instincts.

Graciela: There are moments where I have doubts; what I do is just snap out of it.

Yasmin: You self-monitor. That's part of emotional intelligence.

Graciela: It is. I have a high EQ. We took a test here, and among all of my Human Resources peers, I was one of the highest ranked when it comes to EQ; that's intuition.

Yasmin: What are you doing to help smooth the road for the women behind you, so they can negotiate better opportunities?

Graciela: In my role as a global vice president of diversity, I wasn't just striving for social justice. I was striving to make Mattel better. I came from running profit and loss statements for fifteen years, so it was all about hitting profit levels and meeting the marketing objectives. Then I come into the diversity world, and it was about being better at what we do.

As a leader in the organization, I have a responsibility to really capture the true market potential out there. We need to have people with the right mindset to get into the head of the Japanese mom, the Chinese mom. Really, five white guys can't do it. They need to take chances on someone who's a little different; become more culturally savvy.

Teaching people that—it is very tough. You need to live by example. My dream is there's a new kid at a company. She comes into a meeting and says something totally off the wall. Everybody in the room looks at her.

My dream is for the others to ask her questions, not to dismiss her. "What you just said makes no sense, but tell me how you got there?" It's when we are willing to go outside our comfort zone and take risks with other people from different backgrounds that we hone our own leadership skills and become richer.

Yasmin: Have you ever had anybody, or a group of people, completely dismiss you because of your personality?

Graciela: Yes. It's often cultural. For example, I have a lot of Asian friends. At the beginning, some, especially of Japanese descent, thought, "This woman is nuts." Eventually, they got my authenticity. They are more introverted, shyer. I try to be calm, mindful, and respectful of that. Leaders have to be able to bridge those cultural gaps if they don't want productivity to slow.

Yasmin: Do you believe a woman can be a great leader without being a savvy negotiator?

Graciela: No. Seven years ago, I went into a BMW dealership. This young woman comes up to me and says, "Hi. I'm so and so. I'm BMW's number one salesperson for the U.S. How can I help you?" I said, "I want to see the X5." She takes me to the X5. I sit in the driver's seat, I'm enjoying it, and she says, "You should get this car. This is going to give you the right status." I said, "Lady, if we're talking about status here, BMW should pay me." If she had said, "Get the BMW. You look good in it," I probably would have bought the car.

She should have done some prenegotiation homework and asked me a little more about myself. She doesn't know who I am. That's why when women are in negotiations, they need to be savvy about what they want and how much to give.

Yasmin: What would you advise women who want a career trajectory leading to executive leadership?

Graciela: People tell you to follow your gut; follow your intuition. It's something that goes back to primeval times and that survival instinct that we have. We just don't use it enough.

Yasmin: Do you think most women in corporate leadership positions have given up a part of themselves?

Graciela: Absolutely. I see it all the time. They feel they have to mold themselves to fit the "right" image, but this might not even be real. They think they can find happiness that way, but you find happiness in being authentically you. Am I the same person when I come to work that I am at home? Not really, but I am very close to it. Don't live somebody else's truth. Find yours and live it.

Women as Leaders and Negotiators: The Male Perspective

Now let's turn to the men.

It's clearer than ever that the sexes are interdependent. Neuroscience is showing more and more each day how the male and female brains complement each other (see Chapter 12, "Gender Intelligence and Negotiation," for more in-depth science in user-friendly terms). And while women really want to (and can) make it on their own, we must acknowledge that our male mentors are owed a debt of gratitude.

It was very difficult to find men who would talk about women and negotiation. Corporations see this as a legally hazardous minefield; often, a man would be willing to speak with me, but his company would not permit it. For this reason, we must give special kudos to the courageous men who did volunteer their time and wisdom.

Julius E. Robinson, Managing Director, Corporate Social Responsibility for the Americas, Union Bank, San Francisco, California

Yasmin: Describe how you foster leadership diversity at your company and in your community activities overall.

Julius: I'm head of Corporate Social Responsibility, and I view that as being the corporate conscience for the company. A responsibility of that conscience is to make sure that we are inclusive for both individuals of color as well as women.

In that role I have been directly involved with the promotion of employee resource groups (ERGs), including ones that we've committed to our women executives. Because of my station and tenure within the bank, I have been personally responsible for mentoring a number of women in our company.

I am very committed to ensuring that the rest of the executives in the bank share that same sense of responsibility and are looking for ways to develop our employees.

Yasmin: What does the bank do to foster female career development?

Julius: Women make up the bulk of the employee base in financial services. Our bank is no exception; I believe women make up 67 percent of our staff. We support external leadership development activities committed to providing women with those critical skills they need in order to be more effective in the boardroom. These skills are incredibly important components of leadership effectiveness.

Yasmin: Why do you think it's important to have women in the upper echelon of corporations?

Julius: I think that women bring an element of criticality and perspective that any corporation could use, whether they're developing products or delivering service; that by harmonizing male and female perspectives it makes the strategy altogether stronger and relevant in today's society.

The point is, whether you're building cars or designing homes, there is an aspect of the female perspective that I think is valuable and only improves the quality of the services that a company can deliver.

Yasmin: In your opinion, what do women need to do to advance in corporate America?

Julius: I believe that they should not try to overcompensate. I've seen a lot of successful businesswomen who have really tried to be tougher than their male counterparts. And I think their success has been hard won. I'm not necessarily sure that this is the only way that women can achieve equity in the boardroom. They need not sacrifice their femininity to be drivers in the corporate community. I think that they should really embrace who they are and the unique qualities that they bring to any situation.

That being said, I think that women should not expect to get a pass based on their physical appearance or how they perceive themselves relative to men. I think there is an unequal, if not a higher, expectation for women to deliver. As it is for African Americans or other people of color, there is this implied expectation that reminds you every day that good is not good enough. You always have to be better than your counterparts.

"Always bring your 'A' game but never forget who you are."

Yasmin: As you know, this book is about women negotiating. Feminine traits do not necessarily align with what are considered to be executive traits. For a lot of women, when they negotiate, there is backlash; they become what some consider "difficult to work with." Have you ever experienced—in your organization or some other time in your career—women negotiating in a way that can be detrimental to their own success?

Julius: Yes, where I've seen women really go wrong is when they underestimate their power and become too assertive to the point where it's really off-putting. That said, I think women believe that if they negotiate with a man they must act like a man, and I believe nothing is further from the truth. As I've said earlier, I think women should embrace their femininity and bring to business a wider perspective. Women are innately strategic and sometimes a strategic retreat is the better way to ensure a victory than marching straight into a devastating situation. In those situations where I've seen women really lose it is when they have been so locked in to their perspective.

Another thing is, overselling their femininity and thinking that because they may be perceived as attractive, that that in itself is their ace card that they can use as a way to be persuasive. What they probably don't know is that many men feel insulted when women think men can be led by such primal instincts to acquiesce to things that they really don't think are in the best interest of the company.

In such a situation the woman could demean herself and undermine her credibility and thus the real value that she brings to the table. Men can fail to recognize some important aspects because they feel manipulated; or they discount almost anything that comes out of the encounter.

Yasmin: Do you believe that if a woman is too attractive it can work against her if she's negotiating with a man?

Julius: No. I don't think so at all. If I'm going to be going to a critical meeting, I make sure I dress and look the part. I want to make sure that the way I present myself is professional. I seek to harmonize my appearance with those of the people around me. I am really conscious of the audience that I'm with.

I think women have an opportunity to do that as well. If a woman is going to a meeting with a bunch of attorneys she's not going to wear a cocktail dress, but certainly you want to make sure your makeup is done, your hair is styled appropriately, and that in all ways you present yourself as a composed, capable individual irrespective of your physical appearance.

Yasmin: When you say that women should "embrace their femininity," what do you mean?

Julius: Let me clarify that. I'm really talking about their psyche, the way they see things. I believe that men and women look at things differently. I think that women bring a unique perspective to many things, and they should not lose sight of that and instinctively they should try to use that in a negotiation.

Sometimes it may be structural, strategic, or aesthetic. Maybe it's just nuance; sometimes it's sensitivity. Women can express a level of sensitivity in a way that's genuine and authentic for them and very, very powerful. I think that there is an opportunity to always be aware of that and to use that effectively and appropriately.

I think that's where training, such as yours, comes into play. It teaches women how, when, and where to use that female perspective. I'm really thinking more of mindset that I am about physical attributes. From a male perspective, I think having women as part of meetings and discussions is often an uplifting ingredient, just by the nature of who they are.

Yasmin: What is the most important thing you would tell women about negotiation?

Julius: I would tell women, "You don't have to win every war. You can be very strategic. It may be important for you to press forward only to yield in order to get to the end of the game." That would be one piece of advice. Second, I would tell them not to get discouraged if they're in a situation in which their male counterpart may be less enlightened and may discount their contribution. I think that creates an opportunity where women can focus on other methods; maybe together with their male colleagues they can better position something. Sometimes, it's important to bring a male colleague who effectively defers to you during the meeting. If you address a man who is less enlightened, it may change his opinion if he sees another man deferring to the thoughts and opinions of a woman.

In those challenging situations, it may be very helpful if a woman teams up with a male colleague as a means to set up the opportunity to convey your value proposition, which, in turn, may start to change the perceived value of the message.

Pablo Schneider, CEO, The Wider Net, San Antonio, Texas

Yasmin: Describe how you foster leadership diversity at your company and in your community activities.

Pablo: First and foremost, by insisting on inclusion. It's not optional. It's a core issue of human capital strategy; insisting on inclusion makes it happen. A good way to foster diversity in the company and community is to develop diverse leaders a pipeline and network of leaders—in the short term, midterm, and long term.

Yasmin: What are the strengths you see women of all races bringing to corporate workplaces, businesses they own, or the entrepreneurial sector?

Pablo: One of the most important strengths is in interpersonal skills. And that is not to be underestimated. Many women leaders have phenomenal interpersonal skills, which are a key to success and advancement.

The second area of strength is the functional skills—they are very, very good in whatever area they're in. They bring terrific functional skills to the workplace.

And then the third strength is that they have tremendous drive. When you look at the women in the workplace, in businesses, in the entrepreneurial sector, many of them are incredibly driven.

I think women are often driven more broadly. Meaning, they're driven to succeed in their careers but also more driven to succeed equally well in their community and in their family lives.

Yasmin: Are there common threads among the working women that you admire?

Pablo: They are powerful. They have learned how to acquire, wield, and grow power. They are accomplished. Their accomplishments are world-class. And one of the things that I admire the most is that they are caring.

Yasmin: What do you mean when you say that they know how to acquire, wield, and grow power?

Pablo: There's a certain *fuerza* or force that these successful women have, where they have learned how to become powerful in terms of being influential: the people that they are able to influence, the decisions that they influence, the resources that they are able to control. There are many different aspects of power—the ability to make things happen, the ability to help others advance. In recent years, there have been many studies that show that companies with more women in upper echelons perform better than companies that don't, that's number one.

Yasmin: What do women need to do to advance?

Pablo: High performance, for which there is no substitute. Also, engaging in power and politics. A person could be high on performance but if they're low on power and politics, they're not going to advance.

I have a few other suggestions—recruit allies and sponsors, define yourself with power rather than weakness, build those networks of personal relationships and word-of-mouth—and, then, what I call exposure. That is doing such things as speaking engagements, writing, involving yourself with the leadership and through events—the exposure out in the market, in the profession, in the sector, among groups of people, in the media—is extremely helpful.

Yasmin: Where can a woman learn how to do this?

Pablo: Interestingly, from allies and sponsors. When you talk with powerful women and men, there are always a handful of people who really were their allies and their sponsors, pulling them up and teaching them. It is important that the allies and sponsors—as well as those they help—be both women and men.

Ralph de la Vega, who's a friend and mentor of mine, is the president and CEO of AT&T Mobile and Business Solutions and sits on the board of New York Life. Ralph talks about how there were actually five women in his life who played key roles in making him who he is today. Many top women leaders I know have commented that in their careers, men have played a key role in helping them advance.

And interestingly, there's one subject I'll touch on, which is very sensitive. Women sometimes tell me that women don't do a good enough job helping other women to advance, perhaps due to some competitiveness, turf, or jealousy. The sense that I have also is that the succeeding generations are changing and have a different mindset. I'm hopeful that more women will help each other more moving forward.

Yasmin: I believe the primary reason that women do not support each other is because they do not own their power. They're barely in survival mode in the position that they're in. Therefore, they don't feel powerful enough to bring other women along. So describe the best and the worst thing that you ever saw a woman do in a negotiation setting.

Pablo: The best that I've seen comes from my dear friend Nina Vaca. Nina says her dad always told her, "Take your place"—*Ocupa tu lugar* in Spanish—meaning, "own it."

In negotiations, "it" refers to dealing from a position of strength, not just on the negotiation terms but on the strength of personality, ownership, and power. Actually, that also involves defining yourself with power.

Yasmin: Tell me a little bit about what "defining yourself with power" means.

Pablo: You could say that the best is defining oneself with power and the worst is defining oneself with weakness—it has to do with the person's self-image.

Jeffrey Pfeffer's book *Power: Why Some People Have It—and Others Don't* tells the story of a woman who had been defining herself with weakness, and as a result was derailed and not progressing in her career. And he started walking through a process with her, helping her change her self-definition from one of weakness to one of power.

So one approach is the mindset: "Oh, I come from very modest and humble beginnings. I'm less-than because I'm the odd person out. Everybody here comes from the Ivy League, or from wealth, or the 'in' group."

I've had my own journey, so I know what it feels like to be the odd one out, to be the person who could be viewed as less-than.

And then in contrast, defining oneself with power: "Hey, I'm here because I am strong. I earned it. I worked really hard. I'm very good at what I do. You don't just let anybody in who shows up. I'm powerful. I own it, and I'm going to have at it. I'm going to see it through. I'm going to give it my best shot. I'm going to swing away."

Think, "I'm the unique one in a powerful and strong way" rather than "I'm the unique one in a powerless and weak way."

The strong approach impacts how you go into the negotiation: how well you present yourself, your handshake, and the look in your eye—what you call executive presence, where you're going in with power, taking your rightful place.

You may have the same education, same experience, same community service, same board service, same exposure, etc. You can take two very similar people. And one defines herself with strength, the other with weakness. People choose how to define themselves.

Yasmin: Why do some women succeed in corporate America; what is the secret sauce, the key ingredient?

Pablo: One of the keys that really stands out is the depth, breadth, and strength of your network—a big network of key relationships, both inside and outside. That allows the person to have a broader power base and more options and more opportunities. So let's say that's the secret sauce—the internal is predominant but the external is very important for both the current position and for the person's career.

Yasmin: You're absolutely right. It's critical to have that support system because that's what relationships are. Would you extrapolate a bit into the future? What opportunities do you see for accomplished women with great negotiation skills?

Pablo: I have a strategic sense that women are on the brink of major breakthroughs and advancement in America. The common concern is there are not enough women in leadership today. My main concern is when the dam breaks and massive opportunities arise for board and senior executive roles, will enough women be developed and ready?

What I would say is corporate America is underprepared. I see that we need to dramatically expand and exponentially grow diverse leadership, because those opportunities are coming and my concern is will we be ready as the significant numbers of opportunities open up compared to in previous years.

Yasmin: How should women put their negotiation skills to work in ways that will assist them up the corporate ladder?

Pablo: In my view, board service is one of the best ways to develop and advance large numbers of diverse leaders into top leadership. Professionals can start out by serving on association, community, or nonprofit boards. And then, they can move forward on private boards, then governmental and larger-scale boards, and, ultimately, to corporate boards.

I've spoken with dozens of Fortune 1000 board members. One of the predominant threads is a very long-term track record of serving on various kinds of boards for many years prior to serving on corporate boards.

You've got great performance and personal skills. You've got great politics and power. And externally, one of the best things that you can possibly do is to serve on a board. The value of board service is far beyond what most people consider. And it's definitely worth pursuing as a way of giving back, of creating value, and, also, to advance in one's career or business. Board service is more strategy-driven. I would argue it's a higher level of skill sets and body of knowledge in corporate governance, which involves overseeing the entire company rather than just functioning in one area.

Language of Negotiation

During a negotiation, when we are moving toward informality in order to signal a willingness to cooperate, it is important to maintain an atmosphere of respect. How can we do this at the same time as we are using first names and informal expressions?

We show respect in English in the following ways:

Use "would like" rather than "want" when making requests.

It's more indirect and, therefore, more polite and respectful.
Examples:

I want to hear you talk about that first point again.

This could sound too much like a demand.

I would like to hear you talk about that first point again.

This is safer because it sounds less confrontational.

Use "should," "could," or "might" to remind or inform people about what to do next.

Without such words, you could sound too much like a teacher or police officer.

Use phrases like "I think" and "maybe" and "perhaps" to introduce suggestions.

These words do not indicate uncertainty; they do express respect for the other person. However, it's important to remember to use them sparingly; they imply lack of power when overused.

Examples:

It's time to start the meeting now.

This could sound too authoritarian.

I think we should start the meeting now.

This is safer because it sounds less like you are giving an order.

I'll give you some background information about that.

This is okay if your tone of voice conveys helpfulness.

Perhaps I could give you some background information about that.

This is safer because it doesn't imply that the person is ignorant or ill-informed.

Use questions to make suggestions.

Keep in mind, however, that you are not asking for permission. Instead, you are showing the other person respect by giving him or her a chance to disagree or interrupt before you go on.

Examples:

May we go on to the next point now?

Are we finished with that point? If so, let's go on to the next one.

Use requests to deal with digressions.

Keeping people on track without appearing impatient or bossy is an art to be mastered.

Examples:

May we leave that until later and first look at . . . ?

May we deal with . . . first?

Personal and Professional Checklist for Complex Negotiations

Personal issues may never be mentioned directly but can be stronger drivers and influencers than the professional issues. Separate, identify, and control both by answering the following questions:

Personal

- ❐ What do I care most about personally?
- ❐ Do I anticipate conflict in this negotiation?
- ❐ What are my issues of contention?
- ❐ Do I have any personal feelings, positive or negative, about my counterparts, and how will they impact the way I operate?
- ❐ Will personal feelings affect my professional tone or approach?
- ❐ Am I trying to change something or someone I don't like? Will this help or hinder my company?
- ❐ Do I stand to lose anything (tangible or intangible) that I care about? If so, how can I protect myself?
- ❐ Am I going to use this negotiation to vent anger or frustration? What are the likely consequences of doing so, and do I want those consequences?
- ❐ Am I tempted to blow this negotiation off? What are the consequences of doing so?

❐ How much will I gain or lose if I do not allow these issues to impact the professional side of the negotiation? How much will the company gain or lose?

Professional

❐ What do I care about professionally?

❐ What do I think my counterpart cares about?

❐ What potential areas of conflict might my counterpart introduce?

❐ What reforms or progress might be called for?

❐ Is my professional status on the line? How can I protect myself? My job?

❐ What sources of information about my opponent have I not yet tapped?

❐ What are the things I assume about my counterpart? Have I checked to see if these are true?

❐ Do I have enough power to make this agreement happen? If not, who does and how can I get that person on my side?

❐ What's the most ideal final agreement? The least ideal?

❐ Can we walk away if necessary?

Notes

CHAPTER 1

1. Judith Rasband, "The Power of Personal Appearance," Conselle L.C./Institute of Image Management, Provo, UT, 2000, http://www.byui.edu/Documents/Admin_Offices/Advising/PowerOf-PersonalAppearance.pdf.

2. Maurice E. Schweitzer, Adapted from "Is Your Counterpart Satisfied?" *Harvard Business Review*, April 1, 2006, Product #N0604C-PDF-ENG, http://www.pon.harvard.edu/daily/conflict-management/managing-expectations/.

3. Stuart Diamond, Excerpted from *Getting More: How to Negotiate to Achieve Your Goals in the Real World*, New York: Random House/Crown Business, 2009, http://whartonmagazine.com/issues/spring-2011/emotion-the-enemy-of-negotiation/.

4. "Negotiation: Finding Common Ground," Karrass.com blog, October 15, 2010, http://www.karrass.com/blog/negotiation-finding-common-ground/.

5. "Testing Your Assumptions," Karrass.com blog, July 13, 2009, http://www.karrass.com/blog/testing-your-assumptions/.

6. Karen S. Walch, "Laws of Power 22: Respond to Tactics," posted to Thunderbird School of Global Management blog on November 12, 2012, http://www.thunderbird.edu/blog/faculty/walch/2012/11/12/laws-of-power-22-respond-to-tactics.

7. Michael J. Berens, "The Right Mind to Negotiate," MultiBriefs: Exclusive, October 7, 2013, http://exclusive.multibriefs.com/content/a-mind-to-negotiate.

8. Adam Grant, "Negotiation Advantage: Make the First Move," Wharton Work newsletter, September 2012, http://executiveeducation.wharton.upenn.edu/ebuzz/nano-tools/nanotool-2012-09.pdf.

9. Stuart Diamond, Excerpted from *Getting More: How to Negotiate to Achieve Your Goals in the Real World*, New York: Random House/Crown Business, 2009, http://whartonmagazine.com/issues/spring-2011/emotion-the-enemy-of-negotiation/.

10. "Using the Flinch Negotiation Tactic," blog post for Negotiation Expertise L.L.C., http://negotiationexpertise.com/reni-blog/flinch-negotiation-tactic.

11. "Face Saving Negotiation Strategies," *Negotiation Space* newsletter, November 8, 2012, http://www.karrass.com/blog/face-saving-negotiation-strategies/.

12. "Sales Techniques" tip list, ChangingMinds.org, http://changingminds.org/techniques/conversation/conversation.htm.

13. "Will the Real Target Please Stand Up? Part Two," *Negotiation Space* newsletter, April 1, 2013, http://www.karrass.com/blog/?s=will+the+real+target+please+stand+up%.

14. "Negotiation Definitions Glossary," Negotiations.com, http://www.negotiations.com/definition/concession-strategy.
15. John Wade, "Systematic Risk Analysis for Negotiators and Litigators: How to Help Clients Make Better Decisions," *Bond Law Review*, 13.2, Article 12 (December 1, 2001), http://epublications.bond.edu.au/cgi/viewcontent.cgi?article=1216&context=blr.
16. Chris Hampton, Jenette Nagy, Eric Wadud, and Aimee Whitman, "How to Respond to Opposition Tactics," Section 2, Chapter 35, in *Organizing for Effective Advocacy*, Community Toolbox, a service of Work Group for Community Health and Development, University of Kansas (2014), http://ctb.ku.edu/en/table-of-contents/advocacy/respond-to-counterattacks/respond-to-opposition/main.
17. Sandra Kaufman, Michael Elliott, and Deborah Shmueli, "Frames, Framing and Reframing," in *Beyond Intractability*, ed. Guy Burgess and Heidi Burgess, Conflict Information Consortium, University of Colorado, Boulder, September 2003, http://www.beyondintractability.org/essay/framing.
18. Mike Taylor, "Leading Questions," mltweb.com, 2014, http://www.mltweb.com/tools/articles/leading.htm.
19. Lowell Halverson, "Temperament Sorter Results: ISTP," Family Law Homepage, http://www.halverson-law.com/istp.htm.
20. Deepak Malhotra, "Four Strategies for Making Concessions," Harvard Law School, Program on Negotiation daily blog, July 22, 2011, http://www.pon.harvard.edu/daily/negotiation-skills-daily/four-strategies-for-making-concessions/.
21. "Negotiation Glossary," Karrass.com, http://www.karrass.com/negotiation-glossary.
22. Jennifer Merritt, "7 Ways Body Language Can Affect Your Salary Negotiations," *Forbes Learnvest*, April 8, 2013, http://www.forbes.com/sites/learnvest/2013/04/08/7-ways-body-language-can-affect-your-salary-negotiations/.
23. "Build Your Credibility," *Negotiation Space* newsletter, May 8, 2009, Karrass.com, http://www.karrass.com/blog/build-your-credibility/.

CHAPTER 2

1. Paige Lucas-Stannard, "Gender Neutral Parenting: 5 Ways to Avoid Implicit Sexism," *Everyday Feminism*, November 28, 2013, Adapted from *Gender Neutral Parenting: Raising Kids with the Freedom to Be Themselves*. http://everydayfeminism.com/2013/11/gnp-avoid-implicit-sexism/.
2. Katie Shonk, "Women and Negotiation: Narrowing the Gender Gap," Harvard Law School, Program on Negotiation daily blog, December 23, 2014.

CHAPTER 3

1. Ginka Toegel and Jean-Louis Barsoux, "Women Leaders: The Gender Trap," *European Business Review*, July 17, 2012.
2. Ibid.
3. Meredith the Mentor, "How to Interrupt: Madeleine Albright's Best Advice for Professional Women," Women's Agenda website, Career Agenda/Builders, March 31, 2014 (originally published October 2, 2012, on smartcompany.com), http://www.smartcompany.com.au/leadership/strategy/28278-how-to-interrupt-madeleine-albright-s-best-advice-for-professional-women.html#

CHAPTER 6

1. James K. Sebenius, "Mapping Backward: Negotiating in the Right Sequence," *Negotiation* 7, No. 6 (June 2004). Reprinted as "A Better Way to Negotiate: Backward" in *Working Knowledge*, July 6, 2004.
2. David A. Lax and James K. Sebenius, "3-D Negotiation: Playing the Whole Game," *Harvard Business Review*, November 1, 2003, https://hbr.org/2003/11/3-d-negotiation-playing-the-whole-game

CHAPTER 7

1. Carol T. Kulik and Mara Olekalns, "Negotiating the Gender Divide: Lessons from the Negotiation and Organizational Behavior Literatures," *Journal of Management* 38 (2012), pp. 1387–1415.

CHAPTER 8

1. K. Diekmann, A. E. Tenbrunsel, and A. D. Galinsky, "From Self-Prediction to Self-Defeat: Behavioral Forecasting, Self-fulfilling Prophecies, and the Effect of Competitive Expectations," *Journal of Personality and Social Psychology* 85 (October 2003), pp. 672–683.

CHAPTER 9

1. Laura J. Kray, Jessica A. Kennedy, and Alex B. Van Zant, "Not Competent Enough to Know the Difference? Gender Stereotypes About Women's Ease of Being Misled Predict Negotiator Deception," *Organizational Behavior and Human Decision Processes* 125 (November 2014), pp. 61–72.

PART THREE

1. Adapted from "8 Blind Spots Between the Sexes at Work," http://www.forbes.com/sites/susanadams/2013/04/26/8-blind-spots-between-the-sexes-at-work/, in which Barbara Annis and John Gray's book *Work with Me: The 8 Blind Spots Between Men and Women in Business* (New York: Palgrave Macmillan, 2013) is discussed.

CHAPTER 12

1. Michael Gurian with Barbara Annis, *Leadership and the Sexes: Using Gender Science to Create Success in Business* (San Francisco: Jossey-Bass, 2008).
2. R. A. Altemeyer and K. Jones, "Sexual Identity, Physical Attractiveness, and Seating Position as Determinants of Influence in Discussion Groups," *Canadian Journal of Behavioral Science* 6 (1974), pp. 357–375.
3. M. E. Lockheed, A. M. Harris, and W. P. Nemceff, "Sex and Social Influence: Does Sex Function as a Status Characteristic in Mixed-Sex Groups of Children?" *Journal of Educational Psychology* 75 (1983), pp. 877–888.
4. W. Wood and S. J. Karten, "Sex Differences in Interaction Style as a Product of Perceived Sex Differences in Competence," *Journal of Personality and Social Psychology* 50 (1986), pp. 341–347.
5. L. L. Carli, "Gender, Interpersonal Power, and Social Influence," *Journal of Social Issues* 55 (1999), pp. 81–99.
6. Women of Influence Inc. and Thomson Reuters, "Women Leaders Breaking Through in Their Careers," 2014, http://www.womenofinfluence.ca/advancementwhitepaper.
7. Michael Gurian, with Barbara Annis, *Leadership and the Sexes: Using Gender Science to Create Success in Business* (San Francisco: Jossey-Bass, 2008).

CHAPTER 14

1. David A. Lax and James K. Sebenius, "3-D Negotiation/Playing the Whole Game," *Harvard Business Review OnPoint*, November 2003, www.hbr.org.
2. James Sebenius and Ellen Knebel, "Sarah Talley and Frey Farms Produce: Negotiating with Wal-Mart (A)" and "(B)," Harvard Business School Case Collection, November 8, 2006.
3. James Sebenius and Ellen Knebel, "Sarah Talley and Frey Farms Produce: Negotiating with Wal-Mart (A)," Harvard Business School Case Collection, November 8, 2006, p. 5.

CHAPTER 15

1. "Special Report: Training Women to Be Leaders/Negotiating Skills for Success," 2012 Harvard University, Harvard Law School Program on Negotiation, Report #8, http://www.pon.harvard.edu/freemium/training-women-to-be-leaders-negotiating-skills-for-success/.
2. Martha W. Tack and Mindy S. McNutt, "Women and Negotiations: Unveiling Some Secrets to Success," *Journal of Leadership Success* 3.3 (Winter 2004), p. 70.
3. "Special Report: Training Women to Be Leaders/Negotiating Skills for Success."
4. Ibid.

Resources

Acker, Joan. "Gendering Organizational Theory." In *Gendering Organizational Theory*, edited by Albert J. Mills and Peta Tancred, 248–60. Newbury Park, CA: Sage, 1992.

Alcoff, Linda. "Cultural Feminism Versus Post-Structuralism: The Identity Crisis in Feminist Theory." *Signs*, 13, no. 3 (1988), 405–36.

Ayers, Ian. "Fair Driving: Gender and Race Discrimination in Retail Car Negotiations." *Harvard Law Review*, 104, no. 4 (1991), 817–72.

Babcock, Linda, and Sara Laschever. "First You Have to Ask." *Negotiation* newsletter, January 2004.

Bachrach, Peter, and Morton Baratz. "The Two Faces of Power." *American Political Science Review*, 56 (1962), 947–52.

Bacharach, Samuel, and Edward Lawler. *Bargaining, Power, Tactics, and Outcomes*. San Francisco: Jossey-Bass, 1981.

Bailyn, Lotte. *Breaking the Mold: Women, Men and Time in the Corporate World*. New York: Free Press, 1993.

Barron, Lisa. "Talk That Pays: Differences in Salary Negotiators' Beliefs and Behaviors." Ph.D. Dissertation, Anderson School, UCLA, 1998.

Bateson, Gregory. *Steps to an Ecology of Mind*. New York: Ballantine, 1972.

Bateson, Mary Catherine. *Composing a Life*. New York: Plume, 1990.

Bazerman, Max, and Margaret Neale. *Negotiating Rationally*. New York: Free Press, 1992.

Belenky, Mary Field, Blythe McVicker Clinchy, Nancy Rule Goldberger, and Jill Mattuck Tarule. *Women's Ways of Knowing: The Development of Self, Voice, and Mind*. New York: Basic Books, 1986.

Bem, Sandra. *The Lenses of Gender: Transforming the Debate on Sexual Inequality*. New Haven, CT: Yale University Press, 1993.

Bielby, William T., and James N. Baron. "A Woman's Place Is with Other Women: Sex Segregation Within Organizations." In *Sex Segregation in the Workplace: Trends, Explanations, Remedies*, edited by B. F. Reskin. Washington, D.C.: National Academy Press, 1984.

Boulding, Kenneth. *Three Faces of Power*. Newbury Park, CA: Sage, 1989.

Bruner, Jerome. *Actual Minds, Possible Worlds*. Cambridge, MA: Harvard University Press, 1986.

Butler, Judith. *Gender Trouble: Feminism and the Subversion of Identity*. New York: Routledge, 1990.

Bylsma, Wayne H., and Brenda Major. "Two Routes to Eliminating Gender Differences in Personal Entitlement: Social Comparisons and Performance Evaluations." *Psychology of Women Quarterly*, 16 (1991), 193–200.

Calás, Marta, and Linda Smircich. "From 'The Woman's' Point of View: Feminist Approaches to Organization Studies." In *Handbook of Organization Studies*, edited by S. Clegg, C. Hardy, and W. Nord. Newbury Park, CA: Sage, 1996.

Carli, Linda. "Gender, Language, and Influence." *Journal of Personality and Social Psychology*, 59 (1990), 941–51.

Catalyst. "The Bottom Line: Connecting Corporate Performance and Gender Diversity." Catalyst, 2004, www.catalyst.org/publication/82/the-bottom-line-connecting-corporate-performance-and-gender-diversity (accessed March 3, 2010).

Catalyst. "The Bottom Line: Corporate Performance and Women's Representation on Boards." Catalyst, 2007, www.catalyst.org/publication/200/the-bottom-line-corporate-performance-and-womensrepresentation-on-boards (accessed April 20, 2010).

Catalyst. "Cascading Gender Biases, Compounding Effects: An Assessment of Talent Management Systems." 2009, http://www.catalyst.org/knowledge/cascading-gender-biases-compounding-effects-assessment-talent-management-systems-0 (accessed March 3, 2010).

Catalyst. "Catalyst Census of Women Corporate Officers and Top Earners of the Fortune 500." Catalyst, 2007, www.catalyst.org/publication/13/2007-catalyst-census-of-women-corporate-officers-and-top-earners-of-the-fortune-500 (accessed March 3, 2010).

Catalyst. "Women CEOs of the Fortune 1000." Catalyst, 2009, www.catalyst.org/publication/322/women-ceos-of-the-fortune-1000 (accessed March 3, 2010).

Catalyst. "Women 'Take Care,' Men 'Take Charge': Stereotyping of U.S. Business Leaders Exposed." Catalyst, 2005, www.catalyst.org/publication/94/women-take-care-men-take-charge-stereotyping-of-us-business-leaders-exposed (accessed March 3, 2010).

Chodorow, Nancy. *Feminism and Psychoanalytic Theory*. New Haven, CT: Yale University Press, 1989.

Chusmir, L. H., and J. Mills. "Gender Differences in Conflict Resolution Styles of Managers: At Work and at Home," *Sex Roles*, 20 (1989), 149–63.

Cobb, Sara. "A Narrative Perspective on Mediation: Toward the Materialization of the 'Storytelling' Metaphor." In *New Directions in Mediation*, edited by Joseph P. Folger and Tricia S. Jones. Thousand Oaks, CA: Sage, 1994.

Cohen, Allen R., and David L. Bradford. "Influence Without Authority: The Use of Alliances, Reciprocity, and Exchange to Accomplish Work," in *Negotiation*, edited by Roy Lewicki, et al. Homewood, IL, 1993.

Colosi, Thomas. "Negotiation in the Public and Private Sectors." *American Behavioral Scientist*, 27 (1983), 229–55.

Connell, R. W. *Gender and Power*. Stanford, CA: Stanford University Press, 1987.

Cooperrider, David, and Suresh Srivastva. "Appreciative Inquiry in Organizational Life." In *Research in Organizational Change and Development.*, Vol. 1. Greenwich, CT.: JAI Press, 1987, 129–69.

Crawford, Mary. *Talking Difference: On Gender and Language*. London: Sage, 1995.

Crosby, Faye J. *Juggling: The Unexpected Advantages of Balancing Career and Home for Women and Their Families*. New York: Free Press, 1991.

———. *Relative Deprivation and Working Women*. New York: Oxford University Press, 1982.

Diekmann, K. A., A. E. Tenbrunsel, and A. D.Galinsky. "From Self-Prediction to Defeat: Behavioral Forecasting, Self-Fulfilling Prophecies, and the Effect of Competitive Expectations." *Journal of Personality and Social Psychology,* 85 (2003), 672–83.

Fromm, Delee. "Emotion in Negotiation/Part II: Dealing with Strong Negative Emotions." In *The Theory and Practice of Representative Negotiation*, by Colleen M. Hanycz, Trevor C. W. Farrow, and Frederick H. Zemans. Toronto: Edmond Montgomery Publications Limited, 2008.

Gurian, Michael, and Barbara Annis. *Leadership and the Sexes*. San Francisco: Jossey-Bass/Wiley, 2008.

Hochschild, Arlie. *The Second Shift*. New York: Viking, 1989.

Hollands, Jean. *Same Game, Different Rules: How to Get Ahead Without Being a Bully Broad, Ice Queen, or "Ms. Understood."* New York: McGraw-Hill, 2001.

Hoovers.com. Staples, Inc. http://www.hoovers.com/company-information/cs/company-profile.Staples_Inc.ea9f8fd1ad9009ac.html (accessed April 23, 2010).

Ibarra, Herminia. "Personal Networks of Women and Minorities in Management: A Conceptual Framework." *Academy of Management Review*, 18, no. 1 (1993), 56–87.

Ibarra, Herminia. "Building Coalitions." Harvard Business School Teaching Note, 9-497-055. April 1997.

Ibarra, Herminia, and Otilia Obodaru. "Women and the Vision Thing." *Harvard Business Review*, January 2009.

Ibarra, Herminia, and Jennifer Petriglieri. "Impossible Selves: Image Strategies and Identity Threat in Professional Women's Career Transitions." INSEAD Faculty and Research Working Paper, 2007.

Kolb, Deborah M. "Asking Pays Off: Negotiate What You Need to Succeed." *The Woman Advocate*, 13, no. 4 (2008).

Kolb, Deborah M. "Dear Negotiation Coach: How should I deal with an aggravating counterpart?" from *Negotiation Briefings*, December 2007.

Kolb, Deborah M., Judith Williams, and Carol Frohlinger. *Her Place at the Table: A Woman's Guide to Negotiating Five Key Challenges to Leadership Success.* San Francisco: Jossey-Bass, 2004.

Kulik, Carol T., and Mara Olekalns. "Negotiating the Gender Divide: Lessons from the Negotiation and Organizational Behavior Literatures." *Journal of Management*, 38 (2012), 1387–1415.

Lagace, Martha. "Negotiating in Three Dimensions." *HBS Working Knowledge*, October 2, 2006.

Lawton, R. Hanson. "Negotiation from Strength: Advantage Derived from the Process and Strategy of Preparing for Competitive Negotiation." *Pepperdine Law Review*, 14, no. 4 (1987), http://digitalcommons.pepperdine.edu/plr/vol14/iss4/13.

Lax, David A., and James K. Sebenius. "3-D Negotiation: Playing the Whole Game." *Harvard Business Review* OnPoint 5372, November 2003, www.hbr.org.

McGinn, Kathleen, Deborah Kolb, and Cailin Hammer. "Cathy Benko: WINing at Deloitte." (A&B), Harvard Business School Case, 907026-7, 2006.

McGinn, Kathleen, Deborah Kolb, and Cailin Hammer. "Traversing a Career Path: Pat Fili-Krushel." (A&B), Harvard Business School Case, 909010-11, 2008.

McGuire, Gail. "Gender, Race, and the Shadow Structure: A Study of Informal Networks and Inequality in a Work Organization." *Gender & Society*, 16, no. 3 (2002), 303–22.

McKinsey and Company. "Women Matter: Gender Diversity, a Corporate Performance Driver." Paris, France: McKinsey and Company, 2007.

McPherson, M., L. Smith-Lovin, and J. M. Cook. "Birds of a Feather: Homophily in Social Networks." *Annual Review of Sociology*, 27 (2001), 415–44.

Merrill-Sands, Deborah, and Deborah Kolb. "Women as Leaders: The Paradox of Success." Center for Gender in Organizations, Simmons School of Management: *CGO Insights*, #9, April 2001.

Meyerson, Debra. *Tempered Radicals: How People Use Difference to Inspire Change at Work.* Boston: Harvard Business Press, 2001.

Mulvey, Paul W., Priscilla M. Elsass, and John F. Veiga. "When Team Members Raise a White Flag." *Academy of Management Executives*, 10, no. 1 (1996), 49–61.

Perlow, Leslie A., and Jessica L. Porter. "Making Time Off Predictable—and Required." *Harvard Business Review* (October 2009).

Pfeffer, Jeffrey. *Managing with Power: Politics and Influence in Organizations.* Boston: Harvard Business Press, 1992.

Rapoport, Rhona, Lotte Bailyn, Joyce Fletcher, and Bettye Pruitt. *Beyond Work-Family Balance: Advancing Gender Equity and Workplace Performance.* San Francisco: Jossey-Bass, 2002.

Ridgeway, Cecilia. L. "Gender, Status, and Leadership." *Journal of Social Issues*, 57, no. 4 (2001), 637–55.

Rosener, Judith. "Ways Women Lead." *Harvard Business Review* (November-December 1990), 119–25.

Sebenius, James K. "Do a 3-D Audit of Barriers to Agreement." *Negotiation: Decision-Making and Communication Strategies That Deliver Results*, Article No. N0602C, 2006.

Sebenius, James K. "Mapping Backward: Negotiating in the Right Sequence." *Negotiation7* (June 2004).

Sebenius, James K., and Ellen Knebel. "Sarah Talley and Frey Farms Produce: Negotiating with Wal-Mart (A). Harvard Business School. 907-003, November 8, 2006.

Sebenius, James K., and Ellen Knebel. "Sarah Talley and Frey Farms Produce: Negotiating with Wal-Mart (B). Harvard Business School. 907-004, November 8, 2006.

Shapiro, Daniel L. "Emotions in Negotiation: Peril or Promise?" *Marquette Law Review*, 87 (2004), 739–745.

Stemberg, Tom, and David Whitford. "Putting a Stop to Mom and Pop." *FORTUNE Small Business*, 2002, http://money.cnn.com/magazines/fsb/fsb_archive/2002/10/01/330576/index.htm (accessed April 20, 2010).

Stone, Pamela. *Opting Out: Why Women Really Quit Careers and Head Home*. Berkeley: University of California Press, 2007.

Sturm, Susan. "Second Generation Employment Discrimination: A Structural Approach." *Columbia Law Review*, 101, no. 3 (2001), 458–568.

Tack, Martha W., and Mindy S. McNutt. "Women and Negotiations: Unveiling Some Secrets to Success." *Journal of Leadership Education*, 3, no. 3 (Winter 2004), 63–71.

Tyson, Laura D'Andrea. "What Holds Women Back: New Views." *Business Week*, October 27, 2003, 36.

Valian, Virginia. *Why So Slow?: The Advancement of Women*. Cambridge, MA: MIT Press, 1998.

Waldman, Katy. "Negotiating While Female: Sometimes It *Does* Hurt to Ask," *Slate*, March 17, 2014.

Watkins, Michael. "Diagnosing and Overcoming Barriers to Agreement." Harvard Business School. 800-333, May 8, 2000, http://www.hbsp.harvard.edu.

Watkins, Michael. *The First 90 Days: Critical Success Strategies for New Leaders at All Levels*. Boston: Harvard Business Press, 2003.

Weick, Karl. "Small Wins: Redefining the Scale of Social Problems." *American Psychologist*, 39, no. 1 (1984), 40–9.

Wellington, Sheila, Marcia Brumit Krofp, and Paulette Gerkovich. "What's Holding Women Back?" *Harvard Business Review*, 81, no. 6 (2003), 18–20.

The White House Project. "Benchmarking Women's Leadership." 2009, http://www.womenscollege.du.edu/media/documents/BenchmarkingWomensLeadershipintheUS.pdf (accessed February 18, 2015).

Witter, Dina, and Kathleen L. McGinn, "RetailMax: Role for Regan Kessel," *Harvard Business Review*, (September 8, 2003).

Women's Negotiation Institute. "20 Negotiation Tactics Most Commonly Used," 2012.

Index